...liver's Travels

Open Guides to Literature

Series Editor: Graham Martin (Professor of Literature, The Open University)

Titles in the Series

Portrait of Jonathan Swift by C. Jervas.
(Courtesy of National Portrait Gallery, London)

BREAN HAMMOND

Gulliver's Travels

Open University Press
Milton Keynes · Philadelphia

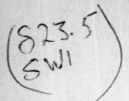

Open University Press
Open University Educational Enterprises Limited
12 Cofferidge Close
Stony Stratford
Milton Keynes MK11 1BY

and
242 Cherry Street
Philadelphia, PA 19106, USA

First published 1988

British Library Cataloguing in Publication Data

Hammond, Brean S.
  Gulliver's travels. – (Open guides to
  literature).
  1. Swift, Jonathan. Gulliver's travels
  I. Title
  823'.5   PR3724.G8

  ISBN 0-335-15260-0
  ISBN 0-335-15259-7 Pbk

Library of Congress Cataloging-in-Publication Data

Hammond, Brean S., 1951–
  Gulliver's travels.
  (Open guides to literature).
  Bibliography: p.
  Includes index.
  1. Swift, Jonathan, 1667–1745. Gulliver's travels.
I. Swift, Jonathan, 1667–1745. Gulliver's travels.
II. Title.   III. Series.
PR3724.G8H28 1988   823'.5   87-31402
ISBN 0-335-15260-0
ISBN 0-335-15259-7 (pbk.)

Typeset by Rowland Phototypesetting Limited
Bury St Edmunds, Suffolk
Printed in Great Britain by
J. W. Arrowsmith Limited, Bristol

For my parents,
Jack and Mary Hammond

Contents

Series Editor's Preface

The intention of this series is to provide short introductory books about major writers, texts, and literary concepts for students of courses in Higher Education which substantially or wholly involve the study of Literature.

The series adopts a pedagogic approach and style similar to that of Open University material for Literature courses. *Open Guides* aim to inculcate the reading 'skills' which many introductory books in the field tend, mistakenly, to assume that the reader already possesses. They are, in this sense, 'teacherly' texts, planned and written in a manner which will develop in the reader the confidence to undertake further independent study of the topic. They are 'open' in two senses. First, they offer a three-way tutorial exchange between the writer of the *Guide*, the text or texts in question, and the reader. They invite readers to join in an exploratory discussion of texts, concentrating on their key aspects and on the main problems which readers, coming to the texts for the first time, are likely to encounter. The flow of a *Guide* 'discourse' is established by putting questions for the reader to follow up in a tentative and searching spirit, guided by the writer's comments, but not dominated by an over-arching and single-mindedly-pursued argument or evaluation, which itself requires to be 'read'.

Guides are also 'open' in a second sense. They assume that literary texts are 'plural', that there is no end to interpretation, and that it is for the reader to undertake the pleasurable task of discovering meaning and value in such texts. *Guides* seek to provide, in compact form, such relevant biographical, historical and cultural information as bears upon the reading of the text, and they point the reader to a selection of the best available critical discussions of it. They are not in themselves concerned to propose, or to counter, particular readings of the texts, but rather to put *Guide* readers in a position to do that for themselves. Experienced travellers learn to dispense with guides, and so it should be for readers of this series.

This *Guide* will be best studied in conjunction with the Penguin Classics edition of the text, edited by Peter Dixon and John Chalker (published 1967, reprinted 1986). All page references are to this edition.

Graham Martin

Acknowledgements

Some of the research for this book was done in the William Andrews Clark Memorial Library, University of California, Los Angeles, with the assistance of an award from the Leverhulme Trust. I am deeply grateful to the Leverhulme committee for their support, and to Tom Wright, the Clark Librarian, and his staff, for making me so much at home. Eighteenth-century specialists 'on tap' included Paul Alkon, Frans de Bruyn, Donna Landry and Simon Varey, and I exploited them shamelessly. Naomi Serotoff gave me constant support and help while I was working in the United States. To Graham Martin, the series editor, is due the satisfaction of knowing that his careful reading has greatly improved the book. As ever, my greatest debt is to my wife Ann.

1. A Voyage to Lilliput

> The act of recreation is not a smooth or continuous process, but one which, in its essence, relies on *interruptions* of the flow to render it efficacious. We look forward, we look back, we decide, we change our decisions, we form expectations, we are shocked by their nonfulfilment, we question, we muse, we accept, we reject; this is the dynamic process of recreation.
>
> Wolfgang Iser

Wolfgang Iser, the leading light of a group of literary theorists known as 'reception theorists', has taught us that the reader's activities are often neglected both by author-centred and by text-centred theories. Reading is not a passive process. The fruitful interpretation of literary texts depends on the 'concretization' by the reader of 'unwritten' aspects of the text which derive from the expectations that the reader brings to the reading experience. On the reader of this book, I wish to impose a task that is not usually imposed by critical books. Critical books normally impart a certain body of knowledge/opinion to a reader who tries to accommodate it to views s/he already holds, or makes it the basis of a thought process that s/he is about to undertake. I want you to read *Gulliver's Travels* with me, but I also want you to 'look over your own shoulder', so to speak, while you are reading. I want you to watch yourself read, to come to understand the basis for the responses you have, to become aware of your own reading procedures. Certainly there will be times when these procedures will be inadequate to deal with the nature of the text. At such times your response might well take the form of nonplussed blankness. Yet absence of response is by no means uninteresting! A contemporary response cannot at once take into account the material conditions out of which *Gulliver's Travels* was written. So it may be necessary, now and again, to say what these were. But the main thrust of the book is not to push any particular critical hypothesis, but to think out loud about the basis for any such interpretation.

Chapter 1

So . . . you have the Penguin Classics edition of Swift's *Gulliver's Travels* open in front of you. Let me suppose you have read the first chapter. Try to describe, as if to another person, exactly what it is you are reading.

Did you use the term 'novel' in your description? If so, what sort of 'creature' do you take a novel to be? What expectations on the part of a reader does the term call up?

Answers to this question will naturally vary widely. You might accept, though, that most novel readers, when they pick up a paperback from the railway newsstand, are looking forward to an invented (fictional) prose narrative, which enacts a 'story' that results from the particular involvements of more or less convincingly depicted 'characters' with a more or less concretely imagined 'milieu'. Bearing those expectations in mind, how does the opening chapter of *Gulliver's Travels* (pp. 53–62) measure up to them? How far do such expectations appear to be met at this early stage? Two particular questions:

(1) Is there anything about the way the story is told that identifies it as fictional? Might you mistake it for kinds of writing other than a story?

(2) How much of a 'character' is Lemuel Gulliver, the narrator? How much access does the reader gain into his inner life? How does the reader know what sort of a person he is and whether to trust what he says?

DISCUSSION

(1) I would say not. The narrative does not present itself as obviously fictional. If it were written in the third person, it would be more clearly a 'narrated' text, but in this case we have a first-person narrator, who alone gives access to the events narrated. As we proceed further into the book, we may find ourselves beginning to question Lemuel Gulliver's reliability as a narrator. At the outset, however, narrator and protagonist are one and the same, and this 'narrative instance' is the case for autobiography, say, or for a travel book, which this writing closely resembles. What difference

might it make to you to learn that Swift's original title was *Travels into several Remote Nations of the World*?

This is a good example of the point I was making that the date and historical culture within which the book was written need to be taken into account. If you put yourself, for the moment, in the position of a contemporary reader, reading the book in 1726, you will begin to appreciate the difficulty in affiliating it to a genre. How was the contemporary reader to distinguish between imaginary voyages, true voyages and fiction? Travel books were immensely popular and notoriously, travellers' tales are tall tales. Some travel books, like William Dampier's *New Voyage Round the World* (1697 – sometimes adduced as a model for *Gulliver's Travels*) stuck closely to the facts, having occasion to oppose the wilder, more extravagant claims made by other travellers. Dampier does so when he rejects stories about 'Anthropopagi, or Man-eaters'. Other travelogues, however, were wholly or in part fakes – some more detectable than others. When Margaret Cavendish, Duchess of Newcastle introduced the reader to her polar alternative world called *The Blazing World* (1668) with its Bear-men, Fox-men, Bird-men, Geese-men, Worm-men, Ant-men, Jackdaw-men, Satyrs and Syrenes, most readers, we can be fairly sure, understood it to be an imaginary world, a fantastic voyage. But what of Henry Neville's *Isle of Pines*, published in the same year? It is the story of one George Pine, shipwrecked 'near the Coast of Terra Australis, Incognita', with four women, who makes such excellent use of his time that he has forty-seven children and by his eightieth birthday, 1,728 descendants. Was this true? In the year prior to the publication of *Gulliver's Travels*, Daniel Defoe published his *New Voyage Round the World* which, although entirely imaginary, has nothing to distinguish it from a factual voyage.

The point of what might seem to be a digression on travel literature is that there is a spectrum ranging from absolute factuality to absolute fictionality, and on this spectrum the reader must locate *Gulliver's Travels*. It sets itself up initially as a voyage, complete with specifications of actual locations and chart readings, as well as a circumstantial acount of the wreck, which impart 'vraisemblance' to the narrative. Even when, on page 56, Gulliver identifies the life-form moving on his left leg as a 'human creature not six inches high', there is still a residual uncertainty – at least for the contemporary reader, if not for us today – that the text is a fiction. Again, contemporary readers might be reminded of unsophisticated treatments of tales and folklore to be found in chapbooks – the small books sold by chapmen for 2d all over the country, dealing in wares like Tom Thumb and Jack the Giant Killer. Similarity here soon gives way to uncertainty, however, as we become gradually aware that we are at no safe distance from everyday reality. Swift's creation of what could be called a 'factual fiction' is one way in which he erodes the reader's confidence, challenging a sense of superiority to, and control over, the narrative. The reader remains uneasily on guard, desiring not to be taken in, but uncertain as to what s/he is guarding against, sure to be betrayed, but not sure of the form that betrayal might take.[1]

(2) Complicating matters here is the absence of any adequate access to Gulliver's inner feelings. Everything we are told about Gulliver is being told to us by him, and we may well consider that his expressed reaction to forty diminutive beings formicating over his body – 'I was in the utmost astonishment' – is understated. In modern critical parlance, this story is a non-narrated story. No narrator intervenes to transmit the events of Gulliver's life to us, so we have at our disposal only what he says and what he thinks. Modern readers are likely to consider that we have inadequate access to what he feels.

It might clarify some of these points if you were to compare the opening of *Gulliver's Travels* to that of a later novel which has a more obviously fictional mode of discourse, say George Eliot's *Middlemarch*. This would throw into relief the absence, in the former case, of any narrator-discourse that would help us to place the events of Gulliver's story, by giving us access to his 'character'. Eliot's novel is introduced to the reader by the voice of an 'omniscient' narrator who makes a direct address to the reader and who is able to tell us much more about the characters than they are able to know about themselves. And this raises a question which I think is worth pausing to put to you. **How, in a literary work, do we arrive at judgements of character? How is it that the reader decides what a character is like, whether we are supposed to endorse the character's actions or not, to identify with the character, to regard the character as 'normative' for the purposes of making moral judgements, and so on?**

DISCUSSION

Many theories concerning this exist, but I find it helpful to think of the process as being rather like assessing personalities in the non-fictional external world. We look for evidence of character traits, which are compounded out of observations we make on the expression of characters' habits. Having isolated a personality feature that seems to be relatively enduring throughout a narrative, we label it with an adjective, and monitor carefully its subsequent progress in the unfolding story. Initial observation may, of course, be contradicted by traits that emerge later and change our view of the character, just as in life, we change our opinions of people when we get to know them better.[2]

Once again, making such observations in the case of a first-person narrative like *Gulliver's Travels* proves to be particularly difficult. We have already commented on the sensory deprivation that denies us access to feelings, moods, attitudes – the more ephemeral phenomena on which our isolation of traits is based. But let's go ahead and see what we can do. **On the basis of chapter 1, what observations have you made about Gulliver's character?**

DISCUSSION

My character-judgements are arrived at by observing the intersection between events and Gulliver's conduct. And I'm confused. I am initially disappointed and indignant about the treatment meted out to Gulliver on his arrival. There are other ways to welcome strangers, even such enormous ones. Gulliver's initial instinct seems to be to co-operate. His 'submissive manner', lifting up his left hand and both his eyes to the sun (p. 57) and his considering himself 'bound by the laws of hospitality to a people who had treated him with so much expense and magnificence' (p. 59) are admirably pacifist sentiments, and may turn out to be character traits; but I'm not sure that I approve of his collaboration with a regime that deprives him of his liberty and has him finishing the chapter like a performing bear tied to a stake. I find myself at times wishing he would 'seize forty or fifty of the first that came in [his] reach, and dash them against the ground'. It is of course a question of relative scale. The balance of force between them is not absolutely certain, but Gulliver and the Lilliputians at this early stage seem to be in a state of mutually assured destruction. This imparts to the prose a precarious balance deriving from contained threat. Of course, the clash of relative mensuration systems, ours giving a man's height as six feet and theirs giving it at six inches, is sometimes comic, but seldom straight-forwardly so. It is amusing, but also dangerous, that Gulliver can flood fertile valleys by urinating. Gulliver's praise of Lilliputian engineers, that they can transport nine-foot men-of-war three or four hundred yards, is serious, but impossible to take seriously.

Concluding the reading of chapter 1, then, I would emphasize that the text generates divisions in the reader. I have a divided response to the narrative, a balance struck out of Gulliver's weakness and strength, his confinement and liberty. His arrival in Lilliput implies

questions about the relationship between the threateningly excep-
tional individual and the state. Single-handedly able to ruin the
Lilliputian economy, to eat them out of house and home, but also a
potential protector and conqueror, Gulliver induces the uncertainty
attached to the maintenance of a nuclear deterrent.

Chapters 2–4

**Now read chapters 2–4, and as the Lilliputian court is revealed, ask
yourself (1) Is there any resolution of the reader's divided response to
Gulliver and his situation? You might look at the deliberations of the
Lilliputian councils on pages 67–8 for instance; and (2) Consider
what relationship might exist between the Lilliputian court and (as
far as your knowledge permits) the English court of the eighteenth
century.** This question will raise a major issue, that of how far a
systematic historical-political allegory threads its way through the
text.

DISCUSSION

(1) Comic-bathetic deflation continues – the comedy of scale – so
that the Emperor is described as 'taller by almost the breadth of my
nail, than any of his Court' (p. 65); and microscopic scale at times
creates the unexpected beauty of marquetry or delicate petit-point:
'the spot [the courtiers] stood upon seemed to resemble a petticoat
spread on the ground, embroidered with figures of gold and silver'.
Delightful use is made of the comedy of scale in the first of several
'documents' to interrupt the narrative surface texture, the inventory
of Gulliver's belongings. On one level, this offers the reader the
child-like pleasure of trying to identify familiar objects from an
unfamiliar point of view. (When I was young, a series of such visual
conundra did the rounds. A simple diagram would be drawn -0- and
captioned: 'a Boy Scout riding a bicycle, seen from above'.) Later, in
the Lilliputian conjecture that Gulliver's watch is his god, there is an
early indication of how effectively the language can take us off guard.
If we condescend to the Lilliputians' inability to identify Gulliver
through a catalogue of his possessions, they have nevertheless perceived how subservient the Englishman is to the movement of time.
In a metaphorical sense, time is indeed his god.
    Yet it seems that the Lilliputians are vindictive, out of pro-
portion to their height. Cold-bloodedly they canvas the various
possibilities for ridding themselves of Gulliver, although it can be
said in their favour that virtuous behaviour, such as Gulliver's
clemency to the six malefactors who had tried to shoot him, can

influence state policy. Ambivalence about this society and Gulliver's place in it continues. At the end of chapter 2, there is evidence that Gulliver has the potential to annihilate the symbols of Imperial power in Lilliput by blowing up the palace, but he willingly, albeit with reservations, subordinates himself to that power.

(2) By the time you have reached pages 74–5, you might have begun to feel that the court practices recorded there – the rope-dancing, the '*leaping* and *creeping*' which is rewarded with variously-coloured silk ribbons, and later (pp. 84–5) the account of the bi-partisan nature of Lilliputian politics – might very well be coded references to practices that occurred in contemporary England. For many readers, there is a pressure behind the detail of practices like rope-dancing, the specificity of the Lilliputian honours system (why blue, red and green silk?) and the reductive binarisms of the High-heels/Low-heels and Big-Endian/Little-Endian controversies, that leads them to reject the literal level of the text and search for contemporary allusions. You will have noticed the presence of various 'documents', such as the inventory and the articles drawn up to govern Gulliver's freedom (pp. 79–80), which might seem to be more at home in a history book than in a work of fiction. Because they imitate varieties of discourse to be found in the non-fictional world, written as they are in a political-legal register of the language, these documents have been thought to signal the presence of an extensive allegory in *Gulliver's Travels*.

I suggest that you pause at this point to give some thought to the critical term 'allegory'. An allegory is a narrative 'in which the agents and action, and sometimes the setting as well, are contrived not only to make sense in themselves but also to signify a second, correlated order of persons, things, concepts or events'.[3] Probably you have already looked at some of your editors' notes and have been led some way towards the view that the text's surface details conceal and are organized by a 'deeper level of meaning', what is sometimes called a 'pre-text'. From the date of first publication, readers have been aware that a version of the events of early eighteenth-century politics is encoded in Gulliver's experiences in Lilliput. Possibly, then, the work is to be classified as a historical/political allegory, in which the characters and actions represent or 'allegorize' historical personages and events?[4]

I'd like you to try out your own allegorizing powers. **With reference to the passage on rope-dancing (p. 74) or to that on the Tramecksan and Slamecksan factions (p. 84), what aspects of contemporary political life do you think are being alluded to?** The following passages might be helpful to focus your thoughts. The first is by the recent historian W. A. Speck. He is discussing the parliamentary and extra-parliamentary opposition to the premiership of Sir Robert Walpole (who many think appears as Flimnap in *Gulliver's Travels*), that gathered ground from 1726, the year of publication of the *Travels*. The second passage is from a contemporary and close friend of Swift's, Henry St John, Lord Bolingbroke, who, in the 1730s, argued that any genuine distinctions between Whigs and Tories had disappeared and the only genuine political divisions now remaining were between the Court and Country supporters, i.e. those who wished to undermine England's healthy, balanced constitution and those patriots who wished to uphold it. (Again, some readers have argued that Gulliver actually represents Bolingbroke in Book 1.)

(a) To achieve their end, the opposition played on themes which had informed Country attitudes since the seventeenth-century, calling for shorter parliaments, the elimination of placemen from the House of Commons, and the diminution if not the disbandment of the standing army. The replacement of the Triennial by the Septennial Act in 1716 [elections every seven, rather than three years] had been viewed with grave misgivings by backbenchers of both parties, and gave the opposition an opportunity to insist that longer parliaments inevitably produced greater dependence upon the crown. As we have seen, this case was strengthened by an insistence that the patronage of the crown was being deployed systematically to build up a slavish Court party in parliament . . . These Country attacks upon the Robinocracy provided opposition leaders not merely with a programme but also with a coherent political philosophy. They claimed that Walpole's system was a gigantic machinery of corruption which threatened to undermine the constitution and to destroy the very fabric of society.[5]

(b) A dissertation upon parties could not wind itself up more properly, we think, than by showing that the British constitution of government deserves, above all others, the constant attention, and care to maintain it, of the people who are so happy as to live under it; that it may be weakened for want of attention, which is a degree of danger; but that it cannot be destroyed, unless the peers and the commons, that is, the whole body of the people, unite to destroy it, which is a degree of madness, and such a monstrous iniquity, as nothing but confirmed and universal corruption can produce; that since the time, when all our dangers from prerogative [absolute power of the monarch] ceased, new dangers to this constitution, more silent and less observed, are arisen; and finally, that as nothing can be more ridiculous than to preserve the nominal division of whig and tory parties, which subsisted before the revolution, when the difference of principles, that could alone make the distinction real, exists no longer; so nothing can be more reasonable than to admit the nominal division of constitutionists and anti-constitutionists, or of a court and a country-party, at this time, when an avowed difference of principles makes this distinction real.[6]

DISCUSSION

Reading the rope-dancing episode in the light of Speck's comment, I can see some force in the view that the passage is an oblique opposition-inspired attack on the crown-ministerial clique in Parliament. The gymnastic feats of those who seek high office suggest, shall we say, the suppleness of their political principles – their willingness to cut capers having replaced any more substantial qualifications for the posts they hold. Precariousness in office, a minister's dependence on the favour of his monarch and susceptibility to changing winds of political favour, is suggested by the permanent danger of falling off the rope. Details like the mention of one of the 'King's cushions' might well send the reader scurrying to identify some particular personality. 'Leaping and creeping' for coloured ribbons continues the gymnastic conceit whereby corrupt and dependent political behaviour is rewarded by a ministry that wishes to put the entire parliamentary executive in its pocket. Again, Speck's comment would suggest an ironic allusion to the manipulation of patronage.

Read again pages 84–5, the account of the Tramecksan and Slamecksan parties. What is being satirised here and how does Gulliver's height function as a satiric technique?

DISCUSSION

The general point is clear. This is an attack on party differences where there is no longer any real reason for them to exist, and as such, it is in the spirit of Bolingbroke. Partisan politics in Lilliput are cloaking the real rottenness of the society, which is a spiritual decay. Surveying Lilliputian politics from his great height, Gulliver can scarcely see any distinction to account for the difference. Gulliver as outsider watches these people play the politician over cabbages and turnips and we laugh at this belittling perspective, just as we laugh at the gigantic pretension of 'GOLBASTO MOMAREN EVLAME GURDILO SHEFIN MULLY ULLY GUE, most mighty Emperor of Lilliput, Delight and Terror of the Universe, whose dominions extend five thousand blustrugs (about twelve miles in circumference)'. The naughtily-placed editorial interpolation of a parenthesis signposts the comic point.

There are, then, clear allusions to events and personalities in Swift's own society. Not only that, but the writing is informed by an ideology of political opposition to Walpole that was in its early stages of formulation when *Gulliver's Travels* was published and was to be more sharply honed later in the writings of Bolingbroke and others. But I wonder if it is really correct to speak of allegory in connection with this work? Certainly, the passage *alludes* to Whig and Tory disputes in the early eighteenth century, just as 'Flimnap' alludes to Walpole, but more generally, the point is that political communities can be cleft in twain by differences that, to a suitably external perspective, are reducible to absurdity. In seventeenth-century Russia, for instance, the Orthodox Church was put into dangerous schism by the Patriarch Nikon's insistence that the altar procession should move from left to right, the number of alleluias be cut from three to two, and three fingers rather than two should be employed in making the sign of the cross. Hilarious – but people were prepared to be martyred for this, because they understood all of the cross-currents of thought and feeling that supported the symbolism. So did Swift understand the real religious and political debates that caused such acrimonious dissent in the period 1688–1720. To my mind, Swift has not tried to represent these events allegorically in *Gulliver's Travels*, but rather invented a community where they could be reduced to a metonymy (a part standing for a whole – High-heels/low-heels as short-hand for two-party politics), a mere empty *sign* of difference. This expresses a deep desire for clarity of outline, for a bird's-eye view such as Gulliver gives us and such as the historical Swift was not able to achieve in his lifetime. The real Swift cared deeply how many fingers made the sign of the cross. Gulliver the fictional persona was at least partly able to be 'above' all that.

I think this point about allegory deserves still more attention, because in my view the desire to read *Gulliver's Travels* as an allegory, as a text whose elements can be given one-to-one correspondence with events, personalities and (especially in Book 4) with abstract ideas outside itself, is reductive and inhibits response to the entire complexity of the work. The first point to make is that several writers have cast doubts on even the most seemingly convincing of the identifications made by allegorical readers. These arguments amount to the view that this voyage does not possess the tight and explicit one-to-one correspondence between the surface details of the text and a concealed historical narrative that is demanded by other political allegories written in the period. Often, it is possible to adduce several identifications for characters such as Reldresal or Skyresh Bolgolam, with equal plausibility. Lacking the clarity and consistency of allegory, the text works in areas of much more general political debate, such as I have been indicating with historical quotation.[7]

I think that even more forceful arguments can be put, which hinge on what an allegory is, properly considered. Genuine allegories are texts which relate to a pre-text (usually the Bible) in such a way as to evidence faith. In Bunyan's *Pilgrim's Progress*, for example, every story element can be reasonably unambiguously related to elements in the author's Nonconformist system of religious belief. When Swift does employ such modes of representation, however, he usually does so ironically, suggesting a lack of the linguistic confidence behind allegory. Allegory declined in the seventeenth century as changing beliefs about the philosophy of language gradually severed the connection between words and things.[8] In the earlier period, words had the sacred potency to be real objects, but in Swift's time, as a result of complex shifts in the nature of knowledge, words were reduced to the mere signs of objects.[9] When we come to treat Book 3, we will see that Swift himself was heavily involved in this process, and was extremely ambivalent about it. Certainly, we can show that for Swift, it was no longer possible to hold any naive belief in allegory because allegory's stock had fallen quite sharply over preceding decades. To illustrate Swift's ironic relationship to allegory, I want you to consider the following passage from his early satirical work, *A Tale of a Tub*. **Of what is the following passage an allegory and what is the attitude implied to the subject of the allegory?**

> Dining one day at an alderman's in the city, Peter observed him expatiating after the manner of his brethren, in the praises of his sirloin of beef. 'Beef', said the sage magistrate, 'is the king of meat; beef comprehends in it the quintessence of partridge, and quail, and venison, and pheasant, and plum-pudding, and custard'. When Peter came home, he would needs take the fancy of cooking up this doctrine into use and apply the precept, in default of a sirloin, to his brown loaf. 'Bread', says he, 'dear brothers, is the staff of life; in which bread is contained *inclusive*, the quintessence of beef, mutton, veal, venison, partridge, plum-pudding, and custard. And to render all complete, there is intermingled a due quantity of water whose crudities are also corrected by yeast or barm, through which means it becomes a wholesome fermented liquor, diffused through the mass of the bread'. Upon the strength of these conclusions, next day at dinner was the brown loaf served up in all the formality of a city feast. 'Come, brothers,', said Peter, 'fall to, and spare not; here is excellent good mutton; or hold, now my hand is in, I'll help you'. At which word, in much ceremony, with fork and knife, he carves out two good slices of the loaf and presents each on a plate to his brothers. The elder of the two, not suddenly entering into Lord Peter's conceit, began with very civil language to examine the mystery. 'My lord', said he, 'I doubt,

with great submission, there may be some mistake.' 'What', says
Peter, 'you are pleasant; come, then, let us hear this jest your head is
so big with.' 'None in the world, my lord, but unless I am very much
deceived, your lordship was pleased a while ago to let fall a word
about mutton, and I would be glad to see it with all my heart.' 'How,'
said Peter, appearing in great surprise, 'I do not comprehend this at
all.' – Upon which, the younger interposing to set the business aright,
'My lord', said he, 'my brother, I suppose, is hungry, and longs for the
mutton your lordship has promised us to dinner.' 'Pray', said Peter,
'take me along with you: either you are both mad, or disposed to be
merrier than I approve of. If *you* there do not like your piece I will
carve you another though I should take that to be the choice bit of the
whole shoulder.' 'What then, my lord,' replied the first, 'it seems this is
a shoulder of mutton all this while?' 'Pray, sir,' says Peter, 'eat your
victuals and leave off your impertinence if you please, for I am not
disposed to relish it at present'.   pp. 116–17

Quite clearly, this passage does refer to a pretext. As you would
know if you had read the entire work, Peter represents the Roman
Catholic Church (St Peter). His bullying insistence that what to his
brothers is manifestly a 'slice from a twelve-penny loaf' is actually a
shoulder of mutton, is a reference to the central mystery of the
Roman Catholic Mass, that the sacramental bread is literally and
actually the Body of Christ. Equally clearly, the passage is ironic at
the expense of the Catholic doctrine. The even-tempered, reasonable
empiricism of the brothers who prefer to trust the evidence of their
senses is faced down by the blustering authority of an arbitrary
tyrant who offends against common sense. Jack and Martin prefer to
accept a non-literal connection between the eucharistic wine and
Christ's blood – one is merely a sign of the other. Here, then, the
passage ironizes precisely the kind of sacralizing connection between
word and object that is the enabling condition of true allegory. We
might say that Transubstantiation is itself the most central Christian
allegory and Swift's distrust of it shows a movement from Catholic to
Protestant sacramentalism that is finally fatal to it. When we come to
consider Book 3, we will return to the question of words and their
significations.

I have dwelt a long time on this question, partly because the
allegorical reading of Book 1 and of other parts of the work has been
influential and is, in my view, damaging to an overall appreciation of
the text, and partly because of the insight it affords into Swift's
position in a wider literary and intellectual movement. Swift was not
a true allegorist, then, because the tradition of allegory was dying out
and allegory writing and reading had become for him another form
of word-game about which he could be sceptical. When he uses
allegory, he does so without the true allegorist's faith in the pretext.

Pat Rogers, in an article called 'Swift, Walpole and the Rope-Dancers', has suggested that incidents in Book 1 can be topical without being worked into any precise allegorical scheme.[10] The rope-dancing episode in 1.3, usually considered to have the most precise reference to Walpole's corrupt administration, actually covers much wider areas of contemporary experience. It alludes to an entire sub-culture of low-brow popular entertainment, theatrical displays on offer in fairs and booths, of which Swift was contemptuous. This view has the advantage that it links Book 1 to Book 2, where such material certainly is employed. Swift was returning, in the voyage to Brobdingnag, to an already sensitized area of the reader's imagination.

Chapter 5

Read the chapter, making notes on anything new you can add to the 'file' on Gulliver's emerging character, and commenting on the narrative events. In particular, try to trace a motif of weakness and strength that plays through the chapter.

DISCUSSION

If you were an allegorical reader, you might be tempted to relate the events of the chapter to specific topical events. Some have seen references to Bolingbroke's securing of the terms of the peace Treaty of Utrecht, and to the Whig backlash to this, resulting in his Attainder. Once again, such readers would have Swift looking back on the events of 1710–14, eager to redress a historical balance of unfairness on the part of the Whigs to his Tory friend Bolingbroke. From what has gone before, you won't be surprised to learn that I find any such reading reductive.

I am impressed by Gulliver's ingenuity in this chapter, by his feats of micro-engineering, just as I was earlier by his miniaturist carving of stools to see the palace. His deeds turn him into a kind of Hercules figure, a Superman, capable of epic achievements in conquering an entire navy single-handed: and yet, there is that curiously troublesome detail about his spectacles. Earlier, he refused to have them impounded by the Lilliputians. Here, they protect this myopic Superman (still wearing Clark Kent's glasses?), turning a badge of weakness and vulnerability into a species of armour as impenetrable as the Shield of Achilles. Play on weakness and strength continues when, on returning to safe haven, Gulliver cries '*Long live the most puissant Emperor of Lilliput!*'. Well . . . yes, but actually, employing Gulliver to fight his wars is not a sign of puissance. Gulliver is the puissant one, and on page 89, his strength is refined into nobility as he grandly asserts that he 'would never be an instrument of bringing a free and brave people into slavery'. It looks as if we should add 'nobility' or 'magnanimity' to the open file of traits we are compiling.

Immediately, however, Gulliver's dominant position at Court is converted to a weakness, as the narrative events begin to shape themselves into a nemesis. Lilliput is emerging now as a faction-ridden, conspiracy-laden totalitarian regime, whose leader's desire for world-domination is matched only by his ignorance of the true extent of the world he wishes to subdue. Gulliver, however, seems willing to collaborate up to a degree. He is now a *Nardac*, seduced by the regime's promotions system even as he is beginning to perceive its unacceptable face. This is manifest in small, incidental ways, as when, on page 92, he sponsors Lilliputian wine over Blefuscudian – '*ours* is esteemed the better sort' (my italic).

How did you respond to Gulliver's pissing the fire out? I find myself divided. Gulliver has saved the palace, yes, but has done so in the least edifying of ways. He has, it seems, committed a capital offence, even if we might consider the statute itself by which he is condemned absurd. We can share the Empress's reluctance to re-inhabit the Palace. The incident stands as an emblem of Gulliver's ambivalent position in Lilliput. Throughout our reading so far, we have been noticing ambivalences in our response to narrative events, to the protagonist and to the community in which he finds himself. You will recall that earlier I registered my own divided response, as reader, to the details of the text. Maybe it is now possible to locate the divisions in the text that give rise to this ambivalent reading response. Gulliver's advent is a mixed blessing to the Lilliputians. Just keeping him alive threatens to absorb their gross national product and their bids to harness him as an 'ultimate deterrent' bring them sharply up against the perils of such contained force. There is in this some of the ambivalence that attaches to the Biblical story of Samson, resonances which intensify when it is decreed that Gulliver should suffer the same fate – blinding – as did the Israelite hero. He is capable of destroying them, but his steady social elevation, together with his occasional ideological pronouncements – an ideology much more liberal than that of Imperial tyranny – suggest a different kind of threat. Is the real danger that Gulliver's moral superiority indicates to the Lilliputian hierarchy that they have lost touch with their own ideological ideals? Does Gulliver show Lilliput to be a society divided from itself?

Chapter 6

I want you to read chapter 6 with the above question in the forefront of your mind. Consider what kind of society Lilliput aspires to be, and work out your own view about such aspirations. Compare Lilliputian institutions with those that you believe exist in Britain now.

DISCUSSION

This chapter retards the narrative to present a static account of Lilliput's institutions. Travellers writing accounts of their voyages would usually pause to describe the various peoples they encountered, their appearances, economies and customs. Dampier, for instance, begins his account of the Mindanayans thus:

> The *Mindanayans* properly so called, are men of mean statures; small Limbs, streight Bodies, and little Heads. Their Faces are oval, their Foreheads flat, with black small Eyes, short low Noses, pretty large Mouths; their Lips thin and red, their Teeth black, yet very sound, their Hair black and straight, the colour of their Skin tawney, but inclined to a brighter yellow than some other *Indians*, especially the Women. They have a custom to wear their Thumb-nails very long . . . They are indued with good natural Wits, are ingenious, nimble, and active, when they are minded; but generally very lazy and thievish, and will not work except forced by hunger.[11]

Gulliver's account of Lilliput is given with even less objectivity. It is hinted that we should compare this society with our own and in some respects, Lilliput will provide suggestions for worthwhile reforms. Positive incentive schemes for obeying the law are features of Lilliputian society. Apparently too, Lilliput's concern for order leads to severe legislation against conduct that we might be inclined to consider immoral rather than illegal, such as breach of trust or ingratitude. Lilliput moves in the direction of what J. C. Davis, in his *Utopia and the Ideal Society* has called a 'perfect moral commonwealth', that is to say, its society is made harmonic by the *moral fitness* of each individual to hold his particular station.[12] Ability is therefore less important than moral fibre to the running of the nation. The educational system is modelled on that of ancient Sparta. As we'll see in Book 4, Houyhnhnm society also owes a great debt to Sparta. It is concerned as much with disseminating pure ideology – 'honour, justice, courage, modesty, clemency, religion, and love of their country' – as with imparting any actual curriculum. Affective ties between children and parents or parent-substitutes are sharply discouraged. Although Lilliputian society is rigidly hierarchical, it might strike the modern reader as enlightened in that females and males are given the same education. In England at this time, as Margaret Spufford says, 'the only group more illiterate . . . than the labourers were, of course, the women':

> The evidence of many school curricula . . . in which boys were taught to read, write, and cast accounts, whereas girls were taught to read and sew, knit and spin, shows that girls were not usually taught [to write] at all.[13]

I suspect that today's women readers of *Gulliver's Travels*, if they are impressed by Lilliput's equality of educational opportunity, will immediately groan at the familiar sexism of 'a wife should always be a reasonable and agreeable companion, because she cannot always be young' (p. 99). They will conclude that even in Lilliput female education is not being recommended as valuable in itself, but only as a preparation for a companionate marriage. In general, I don't imagine that many modern readers take to Lilliputian society, with its disposal of 'cottagers and labourers' in a mere sentence, *but* I think we are meant to see it as in significant respects an improvement on Swift's own. There is no irony being directed at Lilliputian society in its original form, however unattractive the passage of time, and in particular the advent of socialism, may have rendered it.

There are further points I could make on this topic, perhaps the most important theoretical issue being that of what effect the passage of time has on the decoding of literary meaning. But I want now to recall our earlier question about the divided nature of Lilliputian society. My attention is caught by the passage on page 96: 'in relating these and the following laws, I would only be understood to mean the original institutions, and not the most scandalous corruptions into which these people are fallen by the degenerate nature of man'. Lilliput is indeed a fallen society, no longer functioning according to the ideals envisaged in its original constitution. Perhaps it is this gap between Lilliputian society in its earlier purity and its present decline that *grounds* some of the contradictory responses that have typified our reading experience? Gulliver can see beyond the petty tyrannies of this leaping, creeping kingdom and yet he is determined to conform, and by conforming, to make social progress. He has sold his soul to the company store through his policy of non-resistance. Here, reference to eighteenth-century England and to the thinking of Swift's immediate circle is inescapable. Allow me, then, to 'input' some information, rather than to pose questions at this point.

In the English intellectual and political circles with which Swift maintained contact, it was firmly believed that England had an 'original constitution', which had been formed many centuries earlier (in Anglo-Saxon times, they thought, when parliaments also began) and that this constitution guaranteed the best political and legal system that could possibly be devised. Since the 'Glorious Revolution' of 1688, however, when it was decided that by departing the kingdom James II could be deemed to have abdicated, that William of Orange could legitimately be offered the Crown and that a Bill of Rights would limit the power of the Monarch and greatly increase that of Parliament – all of this returning the constitution to its pure form by curtailing excessive royal power – abuses had crept in, unbalancing the perfect harmony of King, Lords and Commons. In the view of those friends of Swift who led the opposition to Prime Minister Walpole, the polity was now tilting towards absolutist monarchy, misaligned by a corrupt ministerial clique who dished out patronage in exchange for political support. Clearly, *Gulliver's Travels* 1 does allude to this opposition version of constitutional history, again not in the form of a consistent allegory, but insofar as it presents a society that has very recently lapsed from an earlier state of constitutional health – abuses 'introduced by the grandfather of the Emperor now reigning'. Gulliver is both critic and example of the poison that is corrupting Lilliputian public life.

Go on now to concentrate in particular detail on the Court Lady scandal, pages 101–3. Consider the following inter-related questions:

(1) Gulliver is here accused of a sexual intrigue with a six-inch high woman. How might you expect him to refute it, and how does he refute it?
(2) What would you say about the *tone* of the writing here?
(3) How does the incident bear on the question of Gulliver's ambivalent position in Lilliput?

DISCUSSION

Let's begin with the significant *lacuna* in the passage. Although Gulliver is at pains to clear himself of the charges made against him, refuting them in exhaustively circumstantial detail, he fails to make the obvious point that it is patently a biological absurdity to suspect him of false play with a woman six inches tall. Adopting the tone of offended dignity – 'vindicate the reputation', 'violent affection for my person' – Gulliver assumes the rhetoric of prisoner at the bar, almost as if he were already before the Lilliputian Star Chamber: 'this I solemnly swear to be a most infamous falsehood'. Since

Gulliver does not actually rule out the possibility of a carnal adventure, the reader is encouraged to imagine the unimaginable; s/he is drawn into a pornographic fantasy of bizarre anatomical unlikelihood, which makes even the image of Gulliver 'conversing' with coaches parading round a table-top seem the most natural thing in the world. Towards the end of the passage, Gulliver's rhetoric moves from defence to offence, as his indignation forces him to plain speech – 'I will name them, and let 'em make their best of it'; finally, the roused Englishman subsides into petulant bickering about social priority. Flexibility of tone, and the movement from narrative time into 'real' time renders the incident almost believable. Again Gulliver demonstrates his interiority to the social etiquette of Lilliput. He is both above the society and of it. His lording it over the Treasurer who 'is only a *Clumglum*' shows his naive faith in social accolades at the same time as the entire affair renders ludicrous the sensational scandal-mongering that was an indispensable feature of the way such accolades were earned in Court society. The attentive reader will notice a further irony when, at the beginning of the next chapter, Gulliver does indeed receive a secret visit from a 'considerable person at Court', having been at pains to deny that he ever received such visitors in this one.

You can pursue for yourself in the light of previous arguments such episodes as chapter 7's inner cabinet discussion of Gulliver's case, to study the ironic undercutting of public rhetoric. Notice how expedient decisions are cloaked in high-minded moral terms: notice how one 'merciful' decision to put out Gulliver's eyes is minuted, while the monstrous sentence of slow starvation is not. Notice that the verdict seems to be at the mercy of whatever powerful personality spoke last. Notice that Gulliver is not properly tried, or given any opportunity to defend himself. Consider what significance might attach to the particular penalty of *blinding*, given our earlier discussion about his glasses (and the point about him as Samson). In chapter 7, Gulliver's critique of courts and courtiers is at last articulated with full consciousness, though his ability to resist or destroy this tyranny is still limited by his sense of obligation to the regime (p. 110). By chapter 8, he has resolved 'never more to put any confidence in princes or ministers, where I could possibly avoid it' (p. 114).

Before we leave Book 1, I would like you to attempt a stylistic analysis of Swift's prose, to satisfy yourself that you can adequately describe its mode of functioning. Consider the paragraph beginning 'it was a custom' on pages 109–10. Separate it into its constituent

sentences and number each one. Try to comment on the language used in each sentence. What is meant by describing the style as 'plain', and is this adjective adequate? Is there any ambiguity in tone, and if so, how is it produced? How, as reader, are you affected by the passage and how is this rhetorical effect produced?

DISCUSSION

'Plain' is apposite, in the sense that the style is unadorned by figures of speech that make application to the reader's senses, or engage the process of connotation. There are no metaphors or puns and each sentence seems to be solid, informative, expressing a clear proposition. To put it in the terms of recent structural linguistics, there is no slippage between signifiers – the words used – and signifieds – the conceptual meanings attached to them. And yet, the overall meaning of the passage, as so often in Swift, is slippery. The overt meaning of each sentence appears to be sabotaged by a latent meaning that barely formulates itself, imparting to the whole a characteristic tone of ironic mockery.

Sentence 1 affirms the solid fact that the Emperor was in the habit of proclaiming to Council his 'great lenity and tenderness' after the Court 'had decreed any cruel execution'. But the denotatory clarity of this is undermined. This 'custom' is scarcely very old – it does not have the sanctity of ancient usage, since 'this Prince and his Ministry' introduced it. Indeed, as the undermining parenthesis points out, it precisely subverts the customary practices of former times. So the reader takes away a sense of a Court that has no regard for history and seeks to make the world anew every day. The subjunctive 'either . . . or' clause further undermines the stipulative clarity of the Court decree, by suggesting a society festering with a plurality of malevolent motives. After sentence 2, which informs the reader of the contrary effect of this proclamation on the population, I find myself becoming infuriated by a hierarchy that can spread such barefaced disinformation. Gulliver's reaction, in sentence 3, hedged in as it is by qualifications ('having never been designed for a courtier . . .') is quite inadequate to express the strength of my indignation, and not for the first time, I suspect the presence of what we might term an 'implied author'. I mean by this the hazy operation of a figure other than the narrator who does not approve of the narrator's attitudes, and who is here in some conspiracy with the reader against Gulliver. The modest parenthesis '(perhaps erroneously)' concedes that if Gulliver did have a courtier's birth or education, he would see that the sentence of having his eyes shot out with arrows was indeed merciful. Yet the reader knows that the sentence is barbarously inhumane from anyone's point of view. The discourse functions simultaneously as an attack on Gulliver for his inadequate rebellion against Lilliputian society and an attack on Courtiers for their willingness to serve tyrannical regimes. By the end of the paragraph, this tension is manifest, as the binarisms of strength/weakness and obligation/rebellion, on which it is structured, flare up into open opposition. The greater expressive energy of the verbs ('subdue', 'pelt', 'rejected . . . with horror') brings the passage out of the realm of reflection and into that of violent action. Lilliput has by its fundamental corruption forfeited all right to the loyalty of its citizenry, but Gulliver cannot emancipate himself from it because he has accepted its rewards. This is the source of the ironic tone in the passage, perhaps best displayed in the final sentence with its convoluted syntax. In order to understand it, we have to decode a complicated double negative, only to find that it expresses a positive proposition that the reader certainly does not accept, even if Gulliver does. The sentence is a useful primer in Court grammar!

SUMMARY

Let me try now to recapitulate some of the main points that have emerged from the discussion. To be effective, a summary should not inertly repeat points that have already been made, but should recast them, or tease out their consequences in such a way that the reader is aware of the ground covered and the *movement* of the argument.

Beginning with the question of the work's genre, and the extent to which it is 'realistic', let me repeat that we cannot confidently assign *Gulliver's Travels* to a genre. If we approach it with the expectations appropriate to the developed contemporary novel, we will make difficulties for ourselves. It seems most like a travel book, but teeters on the edge of being a parody travel book, when its ironic undercurrents became more apparent. Yet it is never predominantly concerned with ridiculing the excesses of travellers, because it is quickly deflected into the description of the actual and ideal political behaviour of a foreign Court. Although the courtiers are preternaturally small, they are not in other respects different from actual courtiers in early eighteenth-century England; fairly minimal tampering with known physiological laws will enable them to exist, so it doesn't seem quite right to call this a 'fantasy voyage'. Although there may be utopian strands in Book 1, again it would be inaccurate to term Lilliput a utopia or counter-utopia. Pressures building up 'behind' the text force the reader not towards any mythical perfect community, but towards Swift's own England, though not with the schematic equivalence demanded by allegory. One recent commentator, Frederick Keener, has argued that the properly appropriate category is that of 'philosophical tale'.[14] Partly because the text never settles into any firm mode, the reader is left in some uncertainty about the laws that operate on this fictional world and is unsure about the degree of fictionality it assumes. This provides an ambience at least hospitable to a comparison between Lilliputian history and that of the reader's own society – the work is not dismissed as pure fiction.

When this comparison is made between Lilliput and England, the major themes of Book 1 emerge. The reader becomes aware that Lilliput is a society that no longer works according to its own cherished aims, and is alerted to the possibility that the same may be said of England. Book 1 is concerned with what the Marxist writer Louis Althusser would term 'ideological state apparatuses' – the monarchy, the court, the legal and educational systems. To Swift, these have become corrupted by secrecy, faction and intrigue.[15] What is important is the way the theme of the gap between pure constitutional monarchy and its degradation is embodied in discourse. The reader is made to experience this corruption through the bespectacled eyes of a traveller whose great height offers both a physical and a moral eminence from which to survey it. Yet the traveller doesn't remain altogether impervious to its seductions, but instead finds himself competing for the society's rewards and even fighting its battles. His ultimate sense of injury when the repressive mechanism of state is turned against him is actually evidence for the extent of his assimilation. Perhaps, then, the reader's divided response to Gulliver is actually grounded in the divisions that have made Lilliput a narrowly partisan society. Its partisan nature in turn testifies to its fall from an earlier, more harmonious and integrated phase of its history.

Let's go on to explore Gulliver's fortunes in Brobdingnag.

2. A Voyage to Brobdingnag

As soon as the reader embarks on a second voyage, s/he will want to know what connections can be made between it and the earlier voyage. Inescapably, the first reading of the Voyage to Brobdingnag will entail an eventual re-reading of the previous journey, because reading the second voyage will be comparative, undertaken with the events of Lilliput in mind. This bi-focal reading procedure alerts us to the question of structure. Of course, asking questions about genre, as we were in discussing the first voyage, is raising structural issues. How, and how far, does the employment of known literary species shape the material of the narrative and interact with expectations that the reader has formed of how these familiar constructs operate? But we now have another environment to which Gulliver the traveller must adjust himself. Is there any continuity between the traits he showed in adjusting to the Lilliputian ecology and those he will now manifest, that allows us to speak of 'psychological consistency'? In other words, does Gulliver's character help to structure the story, or do we merely discover that he doesn't have one? Having already extrapolated from the previous voyage some concerns that the narrative incidents seem to focus, concerns with power and its abuses, with the individual's place in the state, with the Court and its intrigues, with political constitutions and their degeneration, will we find similar concerns occurring here? If so, is it possible to say that certain themes provide the coherence of the story? Bearing in mind that such 'topics' are not themselves narrative elements, but rather abstractions formed by readers paying the narrative a particular kind of attention, we may have to exercise great caution in saying that themes are structures. More tangible is the possibility that narrative elements similar in contour to those occurring in the previous voyage may recur – details, incidents, events, situations. These may provide fixed 'sites' which allow the reader to trace a development in the story.

Read now chapter 1 of the Voyage to Brobdingnag, with the aim of comparing what happens here to the early stages of Gulliver's arrival in Lilliput (pp. 53–63). You might want to list some similarities and differences, or you may just record impressions in a less tabulated way. Don't hesitate to thumb through your copy, to refer back to the previous voyage. Don't be afraid to state the obvious – analysis must proceed on the basis of secure observation of the text's 'facts'. Be on the look out for any imagery that might be salient or pervasive in the discourse. In particular, what is your response to the extraordinary description of the storm?

DISCUSSION

Following my own precept of stating the obvious, I begin by noting that the paraphernalia surrounding the expedition are similar. There is a map locating Brobdingnag somewhere near the region where Alaska now is. There is a chapter heading highlighting the main incidents, common practice in travel literature, and an account of embarkation and storm. Most readers will find grave difficulty in following the account of the storm, and may well find the thick broth of nautical terms comical. Swift lifted the entire passage from the aptly named Samuel Sturmy's *Mariner's Magazine* (1669), omitting only the most technical terms like 'Clewgarnets, Leechlines, Buntlines', inclusion of which would have tipped the passage over the edge of parody. As it is, the chaos of nautical argot is in some way mimetic of the chaos of the elements, but it also opens up a very slight suspicion of a gap between the narrator (Gulliver) and an implied author who, like Ben Jonson in an earlier century, finds the attempt at mastery encoded in specialized trade-talk very amusing. Our earlier textual analysis of pages 109–10 has already made us aware of the ghostly presence of an author figure who does not altogether approve of his narrator's conduct in Lilliput, and is disposed to be ironic about it. The existence of this 'official scribe' or 'author's second self', as he has been variously designated, is reconstructed by the reader even though he has no actual voice and never communicates with us directly. Whenever we feel that his values differ from Gulliver's own, we are likely to feel that our narrator is no longer reliable. File away in your mind this suggestion of distance between narrator/implied author; it may become important.

Meanwhile, we're all glad that the storm is over, or at least that that *language* has stopped! Our relief doesn't last long. When

Gulliver awoke in Lilliput, it was to discover himself immobilized by restraining bonds. As the discourse proceeds in Brobdingnag, I find myself longing for that restraint. Gulliver's unprotected freedom, abandoned by his shipmates and in the proximity of a 'huge creature' is initially more frightening than his captivity in Lilliput because it induces a form of agoraphobia – I speak for myself. Gradually, the reader picks up clues to the fact that Gulliver is in a landscape that dwarves human ecology. I experience pages 123–4 almost like an allegorical pageant of discomforts, more active than in Lilliput: sensory deprivation ('I could see little on either side'), fatigue, frustration ('impossible for me to climb this stile'), fright ('seven monsters . . . with reaping hooks'), arduousness, pain, grief and despair, culminating in a suicide wish. At this point, Gulliver's own reflections must enunciate what is already in the reader's mind: 'how are the Mighty fallen'.

This Biblical adage introduces another major theme, the theme of pride. If there is any critical consensus on *Gulliver's Travels*, it is that the mortification of human pride was one of Swift's main intentions behind the text, and for many recent critics, this intention governs the overall meaning of the work. It is appropriate for us to spend some time considering it, therefore, and to help you to come closer to the eighteenth-century signification of the word 'pride', I would like you to read and consider the following contextual passages:

(a) In *Extension* and Bulk, there are some *Ideas* that are relative, which we signifie by Names, that are thought positive; as *Great, and Little, are* truly *Relations*. For here also having, by observation, settled in our Minds the *Ideas* of the Bigness of several Species of Things, from those we have been most accustomed to, we make them, as it were, the Standards whereby to denominate the Bulk of others. Thus we call a great Apple, such an one as is bigger than the ordinary sort of those we have been used to; and a little Horse, such an one as comes not up to the size of that *Idea*, which we have in our Minds, to belong ordinarily to Horses: And that will be a great Horse to a *Welsh*-man, which is but a little one to a *Fleming*.

John Locke, *Essay Concerning Human Understanding*, 1690

(b) The speaker dreams that his 'good genius' entertained him with the following remarks:

Your microscopes bring to sight shoals of living creatures in a spoonful of vinegar; but we who can distinguish them in their different magnitudes, see among them several huge leviathans, that terrify the little fry of animals about them, and take their pastime as in an ocean, or the great deep.

Addison, *The Tatler* 119, Jan 12, 1710

(c) The Man: When I behold this glorious show,
                And the wide watry world below,
                The scaly people of the main,
                The beasts that range the wood or plain,
                The wing'd inhabitants of air,
                The day, the night, the various year,
                And know all these by heav'n design'd
                As gifts to pleasure human kind,
                I cannot raise my worth too high;
                Of what vast consequence am I!

  The Flea: Not of th'importance you suppose,
                Replies a Flea upon his nose:
                Be humble, learn thyself to scan;
                Know, pride was never made for man.
                'Tis vanity that swells thy mind.
                What, heav'n and earth for thee design'd!
                For thee! made only for our need;
                That more important Fleas might feed.

                            John Gay, *Fables*, xlix, 1727

(d) 'Undoubtedly,' reflected Gulliver, 'philosophers are in the right when they tell us, that nothing is great or little otherwise than by comparison'. It was a truth man had always known. Yet never did he come to comprehend that truth as in the days when first the telescope and then the microscope confounded his vision, when instruments made him feel himself now lord of creation, now gross, uncouth, disproportionate, a lonely mite crawling in a universe too vast for his comprehension – when instruments, in short, showed him man, as Lemuel Gulliver found him and as Swift's contemporary [Pope] described him, 'the glory, jest, and riddle of the world'.

                            Marjorie Nicolson, 'The Microscope and the
                            English Imagination', 1935

Please now re-read pages 124–5, the paragraph commencing 'In this terrible agitation of mind . . . whereof we have no discovery', trying to relate it, if possible, to the extracts given above.

DISCUSSION

Gulliver himself makes the comparison (that has doubtless occurred to the reader) between his near-mythical status in Lilliput and the reduced circumstances to which he is now adjusting. His point about the relativity of all judgements of size (a reference, as my citation of passage (a) suggests, to John Locke, whose *Essay Concerning Human Understanding* was to the eighteenth-century Englishman's mental geography what Moll's maps were to the physical) discovers a vein of hitherto unsuspected philosophical erudition. In his exposed predicament, however, this discovery that man is perhaps *not* the measure of all things, terrifies Gulliver. The *Tatler* extract draws out the vertiginous implications of this sudden shift in scale; there may be an infinity of worlds-within-worlds, a dizzying regress of created universes that renders man's position not central – as had been thought – but marginal. It is of course possible to respond differently to this discovery (which, as *The Tatler* suggests, was made available to the eighteenth century through the new technology of the microscope), and to rejoice in the plenitude, the luxurious abounding creation, to which it testifies. But Gulliver can be forgiven for allowing it to reinforce his sense of existential isolation, given his circumstances. What suffers most in the sudden *Gestalt*-switch that is forced on Gulliver by the inversion of his relationship to Lilliput, is his pride.

Consulting the *Oxford English Dictionary* at this point, I find the following relevant definitions of the word 'pride':

OED 1: 'a high or overweening opinion of one's own qualities, attainments, or estate, which gives rise to a feeling and attitude of superiority over and contempt for others; inordinate self-esteem.
OED 3: a consciousness or feeling of what is befitting or due to oneself or one's position, which prevents a person from doing what he considers to be beneath him or unworthy of him.

Definition 3 gives the sense that pride can be a positive quality – self-respect – or can be a false, misapplied pride. This passage gives us the first overt indication that Gulliver's assumed superiority to the rest of Creation, his self-respect, a proper form of pride, might actually be *false* or *misapplied* pride, because based on a false premise. Can you see how this is relevant to the third extract I supplied, from John Gay's poem? John Gay's talking flea comically suggests this to its host – the man, whose self-importance has swollen, in Gay's accelerating octosyllabics, to V-A-S-T proportions. A sudden *inversion*, and the balloon bursts. Gay's technique in this fable is very like Swift's, in *Gulliver's Travels*, based as it is on the juxtaposition of two points of view that afford very different perspectives. Beast fables employing talking animals are a very ancient way of mortifying human pride, as Aesop's *Fables* had long illustrated. (The beast-fable will be important when we deal with Book 4 of *Gulliver's Travels*.) Lastly, Marjorie Nicolson's work, completed fifty years ago but still standing as a first-rate piece of research, relates changing-perspective satire and other eighteenth-century dilations of the literary imagination to specific technological developments in microscopy. She is certainly correct to say that in the Voyage to Brobdingnag, Swift's imagination has been sensitized by the discovery of the microscope. Just before leaving this passage on page 125, let me dwell on Gulliver's generalization that 'human creatures are observed to be more savage and cruel in proportion to their bulk'. Do you think this is true? If not, does it function as a warning that, whatever you thought of Gulliver in Lilliput (and we found little to endorse wholeheartedly in his behaviour there), he is not to be trusted here?

Read on now to the end of the chapter, distinguishing the 'image-clusters' that figure Gulliver's identity in Brobdingnag, and considering how these images function.

DISCUSSION

You won't have failed to notice that the rest of the chapter is dominated by small animal imagery. Closed in upon by the reapers (gigantic Father Times wielding their scythes, in the old icon), Gulliver resembles a field-mouse on the retreat in the diminishing corn. He is likened to a 'small dangerous animal' (p. 125), specifically a weasel, and then he has degenerated into a 'little hateful animal' (p. 126). Such scrutiny amounts to an identification process parallel to, and even less dignified than, the examination of his pockets in Lilliput. Under this quality of attention, Gulliver turns himself into a fairground act, in order to convince his inquisitors that he is a rational creature.

> I pulled off my hat, and made a low bow towards the farmer. I fell on my knees, and lifted up my hands and eyes, and spoke several words as loud as I could.   p. 127

This can only increase the reader's mounting discomfort. It is reminiscent of Gulliver's unattractively cringing submission in Lilliput, and it doesn't quite achieve Gulliver's aim. He seems more like a clockwork toy than a rational creature and does little to recover the dignity he has almost entirely lost. The farmer's wife regards him like a 'toad or spider', as Gulliver's imagistic metamorphosis continues.

How is this imagery working? Bearing in mind the various extracts above, perhaps you can imagine how this would have seemed to Swift's first readers? One certainty that would strike the reader in 1726 was that as a human being, a rational creature, he belonged to a different order of creation from the animal kingdom. He could speak, he could think, he could laugh; surely he is the capstone of creation? It is true that in 1651, Thomas Hobbes's influential materialist view of human nature as expressed in *Leviathan* had diminished human superiority by arguing that our survival behaviour is 'bestial', closely resembling the predatory

struggles of beasts.[1] Cannibalistic, predatory fantasies occur often in
Swift's writing and already, in Lilliput, you'll recall, Gulliver has
gone through the motions of eating some inhabitants, to terrify them.
In Brobdingnag, Gulliver is in danger of losing his human identity, of
having the distinction between himself and a mere animal elided – a
space inhabited by his dignity. In that event, he might end up as
something's lunch; and on page 130, he almost becomes an infant's
tit-bit.

**Consider pages 128–33 closely, asking how the incidents related
serve to diminish Gulliver's dignity and whittle away his pride.**

DISCUSSION

What is so belittling to Gulliver is the diversity of ways in which he
might meet his doom. He is in constant peril, danger lurks at every
turn and this emphasizes the fragility of the human body. There is a
contingency about his circumstances, his environment is dominated
by the possibility of accident, so that all control seems to be taken out
of his hands: 'If I had taken off my belt before I went to sleep, I must
have infallibly been torn to pieces and devoured' (p. 132). It wouldn't
be quite true to say that he becomes a child, although the care and
attention that must be lavished on him merely to keep him alive does
have a regressive effect. Rather, it is that his adult sensibility is
trapped in a child's body. It has been suggested that this opening
chapter launches four distinguishable metaphors for Gulliver, imagistic building-bricks that are variously combined throughout the
voyage – 'animal', 'toy', 'gladiator' and 'infant'.[2] Their application
to Gulliver's roles and actions is self-evident, but perhaps 'gladiator'
calls for comment. This label applies to the combats Gulliver has
with fierce animals, like the hideous account of his battle with the
rats on page 132. Maybe 'gladiator' does not quite encapsulate the
vein of sheer horror that the story taps, the primal fear that most of us
have of rats, spiders and tiny insects, especially if we imagine them
enlarged.

Before leaving the chapter, spend a few moments on the 'giant nipple'
episode, linking it, if you can, with the closing emphasis on 'the
necessities of nature'. You might refer back to the various scatological passages in Lilliput, for example page 64 when Gulliver describes
his sanitary arrangements in loving detail; and page 92 when he
pisses out the palace fire. (As you will discover in Book 4, excrement
is also a salient feature of the Yahoos' ecology.)

Would you regard such passages as evidence for Swift's deep revulsion at the human body, of a psychic imbalance that only psychoanalysis could explain? Or can it be seen as another satiric tactic related to the general attack on human pride – necessitated, that is, by the generic demands of satire?

DISCUSSION

Passages like this in *Gulliver's Travels* and in Swift's poetry have prompted some readers into thinking of Swift as a neurotic coprophiliac.[3] I do think that Swift was unusually preoccupied with human elimination. The poem 'Cassinus and Peter' ends with the former's horrified discovery about his beloved that 'Celia, Celia, Celia shits!'. For many of us, this evidence of Celia's humanity would not come as too much of a shock. For Swift, lower bodily functions foregrounded the clash between the animal and the spiritual elements in the human make-up. Swift's disgust is also Hamlet's when he says 'What a piece of work is a man, how noble in reason, how infinite in faculties . . . and yet to me, what is this quintessence of dust?' The widespread desire for privacy on the privy (not granted to Swift himself – in the eighteenth century it was not uncommon for people to defecate openly in the dining room after dinner) suggests that Swift's sense of affront at the material evidence of our physicality is not entirely alien to most of us. Possibly, then, 'fixation at the anal sadistic stage of libidinal development' might explain the unusually frequent distribution of such matter in Swift's writing, and the unusual morbidity of his emphasis on it.

Yet no Freudian hypothesis can account for the literary skill with which he deploys it. The defecation incident in Lilliput (p. 64) relates to the wider question of documentary realism. By and large, in travel literature, nobody shits. Even Robinson Crusoe, the century's most famous fictional traveller, is superhumanly continent. To put it more delicately, Gulliver refuses to edit out refuse from his discourse. It may have occurred to the reader that Gulliver must sometime answer the call of nature, a natural enough curiosity. Apportioning some discourse to this, even if it 'may not appear very momentous', is a way of claiming greater authenticity for the story. This is heightened when Gulliver breaks the frame of the text by alluding to 'maligners' who live in a 'real world' beyond the text's boundaries. Suddenly the text gives us a glimpse of its own implied 'narratees', the people for whom it is ostensibly being written. The incident, as well as anticipating the later one when Gulliver becomes a human fire-extinguisher, complicates our sense of the fictional – faeces in Fairyland? The scatological material is also doing the traditional work of the satirist. Traditionally, satire 'holds a magnifying glass up to nature', revealing its objects warts and all. With his microscopic eyes (don't think *too* carefully about the optics of this!), Gulliver gives us a peculiarly literal rendering of that metaphor. He shakes our complacency by providing a new perspective on our aesthetic preconceptions.

There is a third possible route to take, suggested by Carole Fabricant's important and stimulating book on Swift, *Swift's Landscape*.[4] Her book is a materialist analysis of Swift's work and she is not sympathetic to the psychoanalytical explanation. To her, the 'excremental vision' is firmly grounded on the 'excremental reality' of Swift's Dublin. St Patrick's Cathedral, of which he was Dean, was in Fabricant's view an especially filthy vicinity. And Swift's refusal to sanitize his writing, his wilful breach of literary decorum, becomes in Fabricant's treatment evidence of 'a bond of imaginative identification' between himself and the servant class that existed to ensure a hygienic environment for the wealthy. Excrement is therefore a subversive political commodity. Unlike more decorous 'establishment' writers, Swift refused to turn a blind eye, or stop his nose, to what was actually around him and in the broader argument of Fabricant's book, this is what makes him (by comparison to, say, Pope or Thomson) a profoundly subversive writer:

> In the society in which Swift lived, one's relationship to excremental realities was necessarily determined by social and economic class. Not everyone (indeed, very few) could afford to keep these realities at a safe and comfortable remove. There were, in fact, a vast number of people whose entire existence was literally engulfed in excrement on a daily basis, both because they lived in an impoverished, dilapidated area and because they obtained their livelihood by maintaining the cleanliness of the environs inhabited by the more prosperous and fortunate few – by ensuring that all offensive matter was disposed of before it could infect the latter's immediate surroundings or spoil their view.
>   pp. 40–41

To Fabricant's mind, Swift's refusal to clean up his literary act isn't a badge of psychic derangement or even of satiric indignation. It is a form of social radicalism that allies him with the poor and the oppressed rather than the aristocrats of high literary decorum. I don't know if you feel in a position to express any views on this? To do so with any authority does certainly require a knowledge of Swift's life and works outside the scope of this book, but I myself feel some reservations about Fabricant's opinion, fascinating as it may be. Her picture of Swift as the friend of the downtrodden doesn't altogether square with, for example, the proposals he formulated late in life to identify all bona fide Dublin beggars with badges, in order to prevent those from outside the city being a drain on its exchequer. In general, Swift's attitude to the Irish poor was not altogether compassionate. If Fabricant is right to say that Swift was responding to felt realities in passages like the 'giant nipple' episode, it is also true that there is something 'demonic', excessive in that response that is impossible to argue away.

Chapters 2–5

We have spent a long time on the opening chapter, but in so doing, we have covered ground that should permit us to proceed more rapidly. Read through chapters 2–5 now, to consolidate some of the points we've already made. Make notes on the following questions:

(1) **Which incidents contrive to strip Gulliver of his dignity? And how does the apparently straightforward prose style make its satiric thrusts? Consider here the use of 'Brobdingnagian' words, like 'splacknuck' and others on page 134.**
(2) **What significance can you find in Gulliver's being put on exhibition as a 'curiosity'? How does his status in Brobdingnag differ from his status in Lilliput?**
(3) **Try to show how suddenly changing perspectives are employed in these chapters.**

DISCUSSION

(1) This is not too difficult a question. Every incident seems to bear on this aim. Gulliver requires the services of a nurse to make his environment safe and the fact that she is 'not above forty foot high, being little for her age' might help Gulliver to relate to her, but it confers on him a status somewhere between a girl's doll and a human baby. A doll's house, furniture and clothes are made for Gulliver, and the baby-doll ambivalence is underscored by the attention paid to the textures of his environment:

> The girl had lined [Gulliver's box] on all sides with the softest cloth she could get, well quilted underneath . . . She often took me out of my box at my own desire . . . but always held me fast by leading-strings.
>
> p. 138

References to Gulliver's 'box' add another term to the baby-doll equivalence, that of 'pet'; and continuing the animal imagery from chapter 1, some agreement is reached that if Gulliver isn't actually a *splacknuck*, he's awfully like one. There is something very funny about Gulliver's being compared to an animal that the reader can never envisage. The word 'splacknuck' functions also, with the other Brobdingnagian language quotations, as an element of 'presentational realism', suggesting an entire linguistic system, including untranslatable terms and proper names for species that don't exist in our taxonomies. This is part of the process of setting up an alternative, alien world which can suddenly be brought to bear on the reader's own, with satirical effect. Gulliver loses his (already somewhat unusual) name and becomes Grildrig, while his nurse is termed Glumdalclitch – these names functioning, as species names do in Book 4, as a means of 'alienation' or estrangement of the invented world, while simultaneously they represent Gulliver's attempt to become familiar with it and to control his environment. This proves difficult. Painful encounters with immature or deformed members of the Brobdingnagian species (including the dwarf who 'affect[s] to swagger and look big'!) further suggest that Gulliver is a marginal being in Brobdingnag, not able to engage with Brobdingnagian adults on their own terms, but banished to the demi-monde of freaks and curiosities. Dropped in a bowl of cream, stuffed in a marrow-bone, subjected to all kinds of school-playground bullying, his diminutive size rendering the natural environment hazardous in unpredictable ways, Gulliver becomes, in chapter 5, a woman's dildo (at least, this is hinted at) and a bath toy. This is not an illustrious progress.

(2) Not the least of the indignities to which Gulliver is subjected is that he falls an early victim to vicious exploitation at the hands of the Brobdingnagian farmer. Swift's work as a whole displays keen interest in the mechanics of oppressive exploitation and to some extent this fascination with the *symbiotics* of master/slave and sado-masochistic relationships results from his being an Irish writer, and knowing from first hand the realities of harsh political subjugation. We might note in passing that Swift shares this interest with fellow Irish writer Samuel Beckett, whose *Waiting for Godot* is one of the most notable literary explorations of this theme. Master/slave relationships recur in Books 3 and 4. There is also a documentary basis for the emphasis here on display of freaks. The account given in chapters 2 and 3 of Gulliver's being exhibited are very closely modelled on actual showmanship practices, to the extent that dwarves *actually were* carried to the houses of gentlefolks in boxes. One dwarf, John Wormberg, was drowned in just such a container in Rotterdam in 1695. Swift had seen the famous 'Little Family', a midget negro with his wife and children, who did the London circuit in 1711–12. Swift's account is based on known forms of popular culture. But it is also built into the book's imaginative scheme. The

first voyage ends with Gulliver exhibiting Blefuscudian cattle in England; by a process of inversion, he is now on display. His journey from Lilliput to Brobdingnag involves a reversal of roles: from being the showman, he is now the show; great in relation to littleness, he is now little in relation to greatness.

Did you notice that the emphasis on performance turns Gulliver into a performing monkey on this voyage, whereas in Lilliput, constant scrutiny made him act like a hero? It's fitting, then, that through one of Swift's unsettling literalizations of metaphor, the most humiliating event of his stay in Brobdingnag is his being kidnapped by a monkey who 'took me for a young one of his own species'. He is like a performing monkey – so Swift virtually turns him into one! In this incident, the physically nauseating aspects of Gulliver's residence in Brobdingnag are mapped onto the sickening danger of his environment, as our hero, perched on a roof 1,500 feet up, is fed partially masticated monkey-mash by a protective simian parent. It would be funny, if it were not so threatening. The capstone of the creation is dropped on its ridge-tile, finishing the chapter quite literally up to the waist in shit.

(3) Throughout his residence in Brobdingnag, Gulliver's diminutive size forces him to act the swashbuckling hero, cutting down wasps with his hanger. Yet no matter how truly heroic these deeds are, Gulliver will seem no better to the King than a strutting poseur – an impotent anti-hero. Pages 148–9, with Gulliver being accused of cowardice when the appropriate optical instruments would show him to be unusually courageous and skilful, will serve as one of numerous examples. Yet Gulliver's size, while mainly a disadvantage in Brobdingnag, does also entail that he views that society from a unique perspective. At times, this issues in unexpectedly delightful similes: 'I heard a noise behind me like that of a dozen stocking-weavers at work' (p. 129) and 'his eyes appeared like the full moon shining into a chamber at two windows' (p. 135). At other times, the result is a *grand guignol* horror that Ken Russell would find it hard to match: 'the veins and arteries spouted up such a prodigious quantity of blood, and so high in the air, that the great *jet d'eau* at Versailles was not equal for the time it lasted' (p. 159). More generally, Gulliver's microscopic eyesight confers a gargantuan physicality on Brobdingnag – the Queen's eating habits, lice with snouts, offensive odours and torrential urine of the Maids of Honour. We ought not to forget, however, that just as in Lilliput, it is Gulliver's status as freak that provides his passport to high society. His size, so disadvantageous to him, is also what allows him to explore the Brobdingnagian Court structure and sets up the possibility of comparison

between their institutions, those of Lilliput, and by implication, our own. He is both disabled and enabled by it.

You will recall that in dealing with Book 1 we attempted a stylistic exercise, an analysis of a passage designed to make explicit the workings of Swiftian irony. I should like you to attempt an exercise now with respect to the passage on pages 142–3 commencing 'His majesty sent for three great scholars', because it seems to me that for the first time here, the full power of Swiftian irony is glimpsed. 'Ironic' writing encodes built-in signals of its own disingenuousness or lack of sincerity. Some kind of semaphore contained in the writing itself alerts us to the fact that we have to reject the surface meaning and 'reconstruct' the intended meaning of the implied author.[5] If you meet me at a party and I am wearing a glum expression, desperately searching for unobtainable alcohol or for congenial company, and I remark 'isn't this a *lovely* party?', you will instantly detect something in my tone that tells you, as a competent language-user, to reject the literal meaning of my remark and search for a more acceptable one – not very difficult in this case because my use of irony is scarcely very sophisticated. Swift's is a good deal more complex.

Try to bring out in your analysis the indications that irony is present and spell out the operations you must perform to reconstruct a more satisfactory meaning. Trace the presence of the 'implied author' and try to establish what side he's on.

DISCUSSION

There is a structural similarity between Gulliver's examination in Lilliput and this one, except that in the former case, the investigators were trying to establish *who* he was by establishing what he owned. Here, in the scientific way of the biological taxonomist, the scholars are trying to establish *what* he is. Generally, this kind of 'expert' investigation is a one-sided affair; the object on the table doesn't usually have a view to put. When they pronounce that he 'could not be produced according to the regular Laws of Nature' and record the illuminating verdict that he is *lusus naturae*, the reader knows that this is nonsense because Gulliver's transmission of the discourse proves him quite rational and human. And of course, *lusus naturae* – 'sport of nature' or 'one of nature's jokes' – is actually just a Latin tag used by 'experts' to conceal the fact that they have no idea at all what they are talking about. The joke is clearly on the 'experts' and this passage takes its place among many other eighteenth-century satires at the expense of quackery and fake expertise. (You may be familiar with the charlatans Thwackum and Square in Fielding's *Tom Jones*, for example.) Gulliver and the implied author are at one in rejecting theoretical formulations that belie common sense – 'to the unspeakable advancement of human knowledge'. Yet if we look closely at the scholars' arguments, we find them making use of a pattern of argument that recent scholars have called 'theriophily'. There is a body of post-Renaissance writing that enunciates the paradox that, despite human presumption and pride, beasts are in many respects superior to men. They are more 'natural'. One aspect of this naturalness is that they are better adapted to surviving in the environment than are men. Utilizing these arguments, the Brobdingnagian scholars can emphasize Gulliver's fragility and feebleness, which after all quite accurately characterizes Gulliver's ill-adaptedness to Brobdingnagian survival. What 'theriophilists' leave out of account is human technology, the product of intelligent inventiveness, that ensures man's survival in the environment by transforming it; or else they take this as just another indication of man's fall from naturalness. In Brobdingnag, however, Gulliver's technology (his hanger) and his quick-wittedness are fully stretched and he is, in a sense, one of nature's jokes. Gulliver's entente with the implied author is therefore incomplete. Irony occurs at the expense of the scholars, but also at the narrator's own expense; and their comparison between Gulliver and 'an embryo, or abortive birth', self-laceratingly retold by him, contributes its widow's mite towards whittling away his pride.

Chapters 6 and 7

In these chapters, the King of Brobdingnag is a prominent figure. What impressions have you already formed of him? How does his monarchical deportment compare to that of the Emperor of Lilliput?

DISCUSSION

I was initially impressed by the King's circumspection, his careful examination of Gulliver, and weighing of the evidence, his refusal to be unduly influenced by his own scholars. He treats Gulliver with care, but without hostility, and makes enlightened provision for his well-being. The King is, we are told, a 'learned' man, educated in mathematics and philosophy, a welcome change from the Lilliputian Emperor (and notice the difference in title, perhaps suggesting an absence of imperialistic ambition on the part of the Brobdingnagians). A family man, the King uses Sabbath dinner to find out about European culture, in which the Lilliputians professed not the slightest interest.

Look now at the account of that dinner, pages 145–6. Where do your sympathies lie here? Where do those of the 'implied author' lie? Difficult, isn't it? My reaction seems to be subtly modified almost from sentence to sentence. Gulliver is present at the Sabbath dinner – a cosy family occasion, very English except for the estranging detail that Sabbath is Wednesday – and there is something both patronizing and ridiculous in the phrase 'my little chair and table were placed at his left hand before one of the salt-cellars'. My thought when Gulliver is being cross-examined about British 'manners' and so forth, is whether *I* could make any showing of answering such questions. Gulliver's grasp and information must be quite considerable. His sudden excess of patriotism is natural enough and commendable to a degree, though I could wish that he hadn't represented our country entirely in terms of war and division. I noticed that from referring to the King as a man of clear apprehension and exact judgement, Gulliver slips into attacking 'the prejudices of his education' when it is not 'prejudice' but rather 'judgement' that produces the King's comments. It seems clear that the implied author doesn't endorse this phrase, so it rebounds on Gulliver. The sentence beginning 'But I confess' uses what we might call 'grammatical delaying tactics' to create its effect of bathos. As clause follows clause and as the comic description of Gulliver being picked up and stroked like a tame hamster is juxtaposed with the more high-minded content of the conversation, being a Whig or a Tory ends up seeming as relevant to Gulliver as to the average guinea-pig. Yet when the King goes on to concede tolerantly that even humans have their story, reducing human life to a community of ants, I, as human reader, feel *implicated* in that withering condescension. Like Gulliver, I do want to defend my corner; but there is something excessive in the way Gulliver does it and I wish to dissociate myself from that. His rhetorical 'blazon' of Old England's Glories sounds almost like a medieval Knight-Errant praising his mistress, particularly in view of the detail that he is blushing: 'Mistress of Arts and Arms, the Scourge of France, the Arbitress of Europe'. One is reminded of John of Gaunt's famous speech in *Richard II* – 'This royal throne of kings, this sceptr'd isle'. His subsequent actions are equally puzzling. There is the beginning of an assimilation process, a taking on of Brobdingnagian colour, which we saw progress a long way in Lilliput. I don't mind English high society being ridiculed from this 'naturalized' Brobdingnagian standpoint, but I find it more unsettling that Gulliver should be so divorced from a secure sense of self that he can actually jeer at his own mirror-image. Again, there is the uneasy feeling that an implied author is behind Gulliver's account here, boxing him into a corner; and even if I'm sometimes nimbler on my feet than Gulliver is (I don't for example think the only criterion of a temple's worth is its height – see page 153), I seem to be very short of corners to retreat into.

And so to chapter 6. Read it, and comment first, if you would, on the verdict pronounced by the King on the English nation. How acceptable do you find it? Then analyse the dialectical process through which it is reached. (By 'dialectical' here, I mean the kind of argumentative process that produces out of a positive thesis and negative counter-thesis a greater unity, a synthesis.) Do you think there is anything *contrived* about the King's questions to Gulliver? Would it be fair to say that the King is being ambushed as an authorial mouthpiece here?

DISCUSSION

In a sense, the harsh verdict is not unexpected. It is the culmination of a series of vermin images that have threaded through the voyage, identifications that Gulliver has tried desperately hard to resist. His manner of resistance has been to display his 'rationality', to assert that his behaviour proceeds from no mere brute instinct; so it is shocking to the reader that in the end the comparison has been made to stick to man's moral, rather than his physical being. Let's look more closely at the process leading up to this partly familiar, partly surprising conclusion.

At the outset (pp. 166–7), Gulliver is making a plea on behalf of the little people, repeating his rather extraordinary claim that 'in our country . . . the tallest persons are the least provided with [reason]' (p. 125). I am not aware of any equation that states height to be inversely proportional to intelligence. Perhaps this is a private joke: Swift was a tall man. Jokes about height were popular in Swift's immediate circle. In a letter to the *Guardian* published on 25 June 1713 (no. 91), the diminutive Alexander Pope, posing as one Bob Short, had reported that 'a Sett of us have formed a Society, who are Sworn to *Dare to be Short*, and boldly bear out the Dignity of Littleness under the Noses of those Enormous Engrossers of Manhood, those Hyperbolical Monsters of the Species, the Tall Fellows that overlook us. The day of our Institution was the *Tenth* of *December*; being the *Shortest* of the Year, on which we are to hold our Annual Feast over a Dish of *Shrimps*' and so the joke goes on. Atmospherically, this spoof has certainly something in common with

Gulliver's Travels, prohibiting as it does the wearing of high heels –
'an open Renunciation of Littleness' – and making play with the
familiar theory that mankind had degenerated in stature since
primitive times. At any rate, Gulliver goes on to tell us that after his
rather commonplace and shopsoiled references to ants and bees, the
King 'began to conceive a much better opinion of [him] than he had
ever before'. Perhaps, but we only have his word for that. Placing
himself in the tradition of the great public orators of Greece and
Rome, Gulliver goes on to give such a bowdlerized account of
English institutions that contemporary readers must have been
driven to the verge of apoplexy. Actually, every question put forward
by the King is precisely locatable as a question genuinely being asked
by those in opposition to Sir Robert Walpole's government in the
1720s.[6] In the very *particularity* of the King's questions, and the
rhetorical colour they assume, the reader senses that they are not
quite believable as the *King*'s questions, but are loaded with ulterior
intentions. The King supposedly asks whether the Bishop Peers 'had
never been compliers with the times while they were common priests,
or slavish prostitute chaplains to some nobleman, whose opinions
they continued servilely to follow after they were admitted into that
assembly'. We can scarcely remain deaf to the voice of the historical
Jonathan Swift in these stridently aggressive formulations. (You can
refer to the biographical appendix to learn more about Swift's
position as a Church of Ireland clergyman.) The sentiments certainly
match his recorded views on his brother clergymen in Ireland. It is, I
think, indisputable that the King is voicing a set of opposition
criticisms of ruling Whig governmental, judiciary, financial and
military procedures operating from 1714 onwards; and characterization is subservient to the local urgencies of political satire. The
King employs a catalogue of nouns, so typical a feature of Swift's
prose style, to crush Gulliver under the physical weight of his
indictment. Working as it does by accretion, the piling up of noun
upon noun, the catalogue suggests that it can be infinitely expanded,
that there is no logical reason why it should ever stop augmenting.[7]

Now look closely at the final paragraph, pages 172–3. How, exactly,
are you 'positioned' by the King's summary? What freedom is left
you to manoeuvre under the weight of this judgement? List some
of the ways in which you might avoid the cutting edge of this
judgement. Some suggestions:

(1) 'Just as Gulliver initially gave a far too sanitized account of
English institutional life, replacing what is by what ought to be the
case, so now the King is throwing babies out with bathwater. His

account of English corruption is also excessive, so that the reader is directed to find a middle way not given in the claustrophobic set of mutually cancelling inversions supplied. We are neither as good as Gulliver pretends, nor as evil as the King suspects.'

(2) 'A current political motto, promulgated by the Roman historian Polybius, held that "the corruptions of the best things are the worst". Again emphasizing the theme of degeneration from an uncorrupted original foundation (a theme present in Gulliver's critique of Lilliput), the King does point the way towards a return to former constitutional purity. He shows how to diminish the distance between a good man and a good office-holder. Moral, rather than practical qualification for office suggests a route back to constitutional health. Despite appearances, then, his attack is helpful, constructive, even cause for optimism.'

(3) 'There is a space left by the King for at least some individuals to be exceptions to the general rule of viciousness. He seems to speak kindly to his "little friend Grildrig". I, as reader, can opt to occupy that space. Maybe most humans are as the King says they are, but I'm not.'

Now read chapter 7, to page 176 – 'whole race of politicians put together'. Two questions:

(1) How does Gulliver's response to Brobdingnagian censure compare to the options you or I listed?
(2) How do you view the relationship between implied author and narrator developing in these paragraphs?

DISCUSSION

(1) Noticeably, Gulliver does not take up any of my listed options. His remarks on page 173 suggest that, despite his rather unctuously professing 'extreme love of truth', he has actually doctored the evidence *in our favour*. If anything, then, the King's verdict is too lenient. So much for my first suggestion. (Notice, by the way, the unattractive pomposity of Gulliver's allying himself with the historian Dionysius, and of his filial piety towards his 'political mother'.) However, in the next paragraph, on page 174, Gulliver seems to *reject altogether* the validity of the King's analysis, another option that didn't occur to me. And look how he does it. Assuming the arch worldliness of one who has lived much in 'polite' society, Gulliver condescends to the King as if he were a callow country

bumpkin whose rustic moralizing could only produce in fashionable society a languid yawn.

(2) As an example of the King's 'confined education', Gulliver tells the story of his offering the secret of gunpowder to the King, a story that, as Gulliver says, 'will hardly obtain belief' – but not for the reasons he has in mind! Gulliver, it seems, is a changed man. This is the man who, in Lilliput, refused to 'be an instrument of bringing a free and grave people into slavery' (p. 89), now taking unbridled delight in delivering bloodthirsty cameos of war to an astonished Brobdingnagian pacifist. Gulliver's set of 'magic lantern' slides of war are attractively repulsive, if I may so put it. Obviously, though, Gulliver has by now entirely lost authorial endorsement. In Lilliput, as we argued, Gulliver's actions gain a considerable measure of authorial backing, even if there is never a complete identification between implied author and narrator. By now, that backing has been entirely withdrawn and there is no longer any reliability in Gulliver's observation of his environment. Far from being the scalpel employed to dissect a cancerous society, as he was in Lilliput, Gulliver – his nation's ambassador – is now the corpse. When the King makes his impressively concise and trenchant condemnation of Gulliver, calling him an 'impotent and grovelling insect' (p. 175), I now wish to applaud him to the echo, although I resisted that earlier. In the next paragraph, Gulliver gives himself away at every turn. If a Prince has secured the 'veneration, love, and esteem' of his people, why should he seek to become 'absolute master' of their lives, liberties and fortunes? Gulliver's own absolutist leanings are made apparent here and since he presumes to speak for the 'English reader', *this* English reader is trying hard to dissociate himself from Gulliver at the same time as he is forced to recognize the limits of dissociation. However much I might despise the pseudo-complexity of government bureaucracy, however much I might long for the King's primitive, arcadian definition of government – to make two ears of corn grow where one grew before – I *cannot* altogether side with the King because I can see no immediate possibility of this quasi-utopian view of government being adequate to govern my own society. As reader, I feel myself cast out in the cold, wishing to avoid being identified too closely with the narrator, but not being able to repose warmly in the implied narrator's bosom, who, I sense, is now behind the King of Brobdingnag. I'm trapped by my own liberalism into rejecting Gulliver's warlike means of gaining absolute power, but without absolute power, I can't envisage any ruler being able to resolve the conflicts of interest that are bound to arise in any genuine society. I'm too pessimistic to accept that a charismatic

ruler like the King of Brobdingnag can hold sway through example alone.

I have referred to the King's view as quasi-utopian and I think 'utopia' is a term that will bear more inspection. **Read now the rest of the chapter and consider whether you would wish to call Brobdingnag an 'utopia'. We can work, in the meantime, with the OED's definition of 'utopia' as 'a place, state or condition ideally perfect in respect of politics, laws, customs, and conditions'.**

DISCUSSION

One's answer will depend on what a 'utopia' is taken to be. No-one could call Brobdingnag a perfectly functioning society. The farmer's unconscionable rapacity in exploiting Gulliver for economic gain and selling him at a profit; the existence in Brobdingnag of beggars, cancerous women, men with wens and wooden legs, all lice-infested (pp. 151–2), malicious dwarves and the like; and the need for public executions, does not altogether suggest a society whose material resources are plentiful and ideally distributed. Brobdingnag is not an ideal society. It is more fortunate than England in having an enlightened monarch who is committed to practice rather than theory, to peace rather than war; an educational and legal system that avoids division and disharmony by avoiding complexity, and a citizen militia rather than a sinister standing army of paid mercenaries. For the reader, it's difficult to see how all this enlightenment actually translates into social action and, as I've said, if the condition of Brobdingnagian agricultural and urban owners and workers is anything to go by, it *doesn't*. Brobdingnag lacks the programmatic exhaustiveness of a work like More's *Utopia*, in which every aspect of civil, religious and domestic life is governed by a vision of perfect order. Reading *Utopia*, one can see the work being addressed to a particular evil, that of the existence of private property. The Voyage to Brobdingnag lacks any central political objective. It is a divided society and the account given of its institutions is very sketchy. I agree with Robert C. Elliott, who concludes that 'Brobdingnag is supra-human only in physical size, not in moral stature or political achievement; it is not an ideal, in the sense of a perfect, state – by no means as ideal, for example, as the England Gulliver has pictured'.[8] We will come back to this question when discussing Book 4.

Before proceeding to the final chapter, I want to pause on the issue of Gulliver's 'character'. Above, I pointed out a contradiction between Gulliver's noble conduct in Lilliput and the extreme pragmatism of his conduct in Brobdingnag. How do you reconcile this seeming inconsistency in his character? Think about it, then consider the three opinions from critics that I have cited below.

(a) What happens is far more important in its own right than the fact that it happens to Gulliver . . . If the reader tries to gratify himself by completing Gulliver, tries to add intimations of character, soul, feeling, depth, then he convicts himself; he is a sentimentalist, Swift's favourite butt.   Denis Donoghue, 1969

(b) Gulliver has been, throughout, a figure whose behaviour could be manipulated by Swift to suit the requirements of his satire. A man, or a consistently-drawn, psychologically-explored representation of a man, can go mad [as some critics think Gulliver does in Book 4]: a satirical device cannot. Gulliver's behaviour at home, like his behaviour in the audience with the King of Brobdingnag, cannot be satisfactorily explained in psychological terms, because it is a satirical manoeuvre . . . The danger of imposing on *Gulliver's Travels* modern critical ideas of unity and consistency . . . is that, besides obscuring the brilliant variety of Swift's satirical methods, it may blunt the edge of the satire by explaining away some of the violence in terms of Gulliver's character.   Charles Peake, 1971

(c) Gulliver, it has often been said, lacks enough plausibility as a character to satisfy the requirements of realistic fiction. *Gulliver's Travels* is decidedly not a novel. On the other hand, a certain semblance of characterization attaches to this odd hero and narrator, who has local habitations and in other respects is not inhuman. If . . . one allows Gulliver to be a character to the extent that he brings realities to mind – if one will suspend awhile the extreme opinion that, because he is not a novel character, he has no character at all – one will not find oneself set apart from all able readers of the *Travels*.   Frederick M. Keener, 1983[9]

All of these critics have reservations about calling Gulliver a 'character'. Actually, as Keener recognizes, it is very difficult to avoid doing so. We can't altogether prevent ourselves from ascribing to him reason, feelings, imagination, emotions, as if he were a human being. Most critics, Donoghue included, find themselves doing so. Keener's solution – that it is all a matter of deciding what kind of literary artefact he's a character *in* (in his view, the 'philosophical tale') does not seem to be more satisfactory. Our discussion of genre in Book 1 suggested such a mixture that it seems hopeless to try to define a genre which will encapsulate the entire work. Even if Keener were right that *Gulliver's Travels* is a philosophical tale, can characters in philosophical tales be champions of freedom in one part, and of enslavement backed by firepower in another? What does his phrase 'brings realities to mind' mean? Charles Peake's view seems most convincing to me. Gulliver does seem to be different in Brobdingnag from Lilliput and I don't think the differences are accounted for by the effects of a different environment on the same personality. In the second voyage, implied authorial backing is withdrawn, making the character a target of criticisms for which he was previously a conduit. Subordinating character to *function*, the implied author's main concern is to put across a view of the relationship between an existing society and other societies that use the former as a starting-point, but modify it in various ways. Gulliver's behaviour is determined more by these needs than by any sense that he has a 'central core of being', whose integrity survives its environment intact.

Continue now and read chapter 8. Then consider the following questions:

(1) Discuss the theme of 'imprisonment' that is underlined in this chapter. You might look back to page 144 and to page 152, to examine the various conveyances by means of which Gulliver is transported.
(2) Consider the function of Captain Wilcocks in the story. Why is this named character introduced, and how does his action modify the verdict on humanity pronounced by the King of Brobdingnag?
(3) Comment, if you can, on Wilcocks's comparison of Gulliver to Phaethon (p. 190). If you don't know the allusion, consult a dictionary of classical mythology.

DISCUSSION

(1) Reading Gulliver's sojourn in Lilliput, I traced the operation of a binary opposition between weakness and strength that was partly responsible for creating a contradictory reading experience. I might also have chosen to dwell on liberty and confinement as key concepts that organize our reading of the text, since the term 'liberty' is employed so often in Lilliput and since Gulliver's freedom is so often circumscribed there. In Brobdingnag, the question also arises, in somewhat modified form. Examining my emotional reactions to the text, I felt a desire, at the outset, to get Gulliver under *protection* from the vastness of the country, to hive off a space proportional to his size and needs. Initially there is a need to care for him, and the various 'boxes' in which he is transported, including the one that answers more to his dignity by being self-designed and custom-built, guarantee his survival. As his stay lengthens, however, his living-space becomes increasingly parodic. He makes the grand tour of Brobdingnag, surveying the countryside from the confines of a specially contrived 'travelling closet' that Glumdalclitch carries on her lap. Eventually, the box even fails to discharge its security

function as Gulliver, despite being in a box within a box, is vulnerable to the monkey's curiosity. By the opening of chapter 8, what has been a 'caring' environment has become an imprisoning one. Of the King's eugenic intentions, Gulliver protests that 'I think I should have died rather than undergone the disgrace of leaving a posterity to be kept in cages like tame canary birds'. Animal imagery again epitomizes his disabled condition. It is with much relief that the reader contemplates Gulliver's quite literal 'flight' from Brobdingnag. [There is a much bigger point here. Images of confinement and of flight are central organizing images in the literature of this period.[10] To Swift especially, images of confinement have a privileged significance. Hopewell R. Selby has written an interesting article in which she says that 'Swift's fictions of confinement express his anxieties about what he views as the human personality's inevitable tendency toward violent and anarchic disintegration . . . Swift's fear that all restraints, be they those of the madman's straitjacket, the tenets of religious belief, or the discipline of literary 'form', are ineffective checks on the frenzied fragmentation that characterizes modern sensibility.'[11]]

(2) I am initially quite surprised that Wilcocks is as *good* a man as he is. Like John Biddel, the seaman who rescues Gulliver from Lilliput, Wilcocks is a very civil man, an excellent advertisement for the human race and the English nation. He behaves towards Gulliver in the manner prescribed by Christianity, allowing Gulliver to '*turn in* upon his own bed', and taking every measure to secure his comfort. On the level of textual authenticity, Wilcocks is there to secure the reader's belief. If such a man as *this* can accept Gulliver's story (and he also has seen the evidence), so should we. But Wilcocks also functions as a touchstone for a final judgement on what Gulliver has learned from his experiences in Brobdingnag. Gulliver's peculiar loss of perspective – 'while I was in that Prince's country, I could never endure to look in a glass after mine eyes had been accustomed to such prodigious objects, because the comparison gave me so despicable a conceit of myself' (p. 189) – continued in his 'looking down on' his own family, is indexical to his enduring pride. Gulliver's pride is thrown into relief by the unaffected decency of Wilcocks. In Brobdingnag, Gulliver has been a poor advertisement for Englishmen. In Wilcocks, the implied author mitigates the severity of his attack on the English, or at least puts it into perspective. Notice too that in this chapter, the text's habit of anticipating and dumbfounding the reader continues. On page 189, Gulliver responds to Wilcocks's suggestion that he publish his memoirs with a testy dismissal. What is it, then, that we are reading? Whatever it is, if the reader is inclined to

discount it as the most incredible of fantastic voyages, the objection is pre-empted by Gulliver's assertion that it is positively humdrum by comparison to most of the travel-liars whose stories are imposed upon us as truth. Once again, the reader experiences that Swiftian earth-tremor shaking the solid ground beneath his feet.

(3) The comparison that Wilcocks draws between Gulliver and Phaethon finally underlines the theme of humbling human pride that has connected many of the narrative incidents. Here is an extract from William King's account of the Phaethon story, written in 1711:

> The Youth presently ask'd leave to govern his [father, Apollo the Sun god's] Chariot for one Day: The Father's Surprize and Grief were inexpressible; however, being oblig'd to submit to his Son's Obstinacy and Rashness, he put him into the Chariot with all the most necessary and tender Precautions imaginable, but the Horses not finding their usual Conducter, took Head, and the Charioteer became dazled with the Light above, and frighten'd with the Abyss that he saw beneath him, and terrify'd by the *Scorpion*, let go his Reins, lost his Way, and had burnt one half of the World, and froze up the other, if *Jupiter* had not struck him with a Thunderbolt into the River *Eridanus*.[12]

Except that Phaethon is a by-word for overweening pride and presumptuousness, known to eighteenth-century readers through the account given by Ovid in the *Metamorphoses*, which George Sandys had versified memorably about a century previously, the story is not especially apt to Gulliver's predicament. Wilcocks makes the comparison in the context of ribbing him about his big ideas, and it is not surprising that Gulliver 'did not much admire the conceit' (p. 190).

SUMMARY

In summarizing this reading of the Voyage to Brobdingnag, the main point is to locate it with respect to the first voyage. Clearly, there is a formal parallelism at work. Gulliver departs, arrives in an unknown territory conveniently inaccessible to the rest of the world, is entrapped by the natives but by virtue of his freakish uniqueness gains a measure of liberty as a Court favourite. Operating on this formal similarity is a principle of *inversion*, or inverted perspective. Physical size in Lilliput is also moral elevation, so that Gulliver is able to expose Lilliput's corruption and degeneration from an earlier state of constitutional purity. In Brobdingnag, Gulliver's physical diminution is also moral shrinkage. The discourse embeds an arrangement of images and incidents which elides the difference between a man and a *splacknuck*. As it gradually withdraws approval from the narrator, the discourse creates Gulliver as the victim rather than the vehicle of the satire. This serves to whittle away anthropocentric (i.e. human-directed) pride of place in the universe. In Brobdingnag, Gulliver commits the solecism of offering the secret of gunpowder to a pacifist, non-imperialistic monarch who rules by consent and love of his people over a kingdom whose institutions appear to be run constitutionally. Structurally parallel to the solecism he is accused of committing in Lilliput, seducing the Court lady, this occurrence marks the maximum distance between Gulliver and the implied author. Perhaps the major *difference* between the voyages is that the second sets Gulliver up as a spokesman for his nation, so that the reader is heavily implicated in the King's Androphobia. S/he cannot remain aloof, as it is possible to do in Lilliput. If we choose to dissociate ourselves from Gulliver, it is far from clear that the King would care to have us as allies. No corner of the cornfield is left.

In my view, Swift's eyes are as firmly fixed on England in Brobdingnag as they were in Lilliput. The voyage to Lilliput is projected upon an understanding of English political realities around the time of composition. Lilliput takes as its starting-point the practical politics of England in the early eighteenth century, seen from the viewpoint of an uninvolved outsider. Brobdingnag is projected upon the same understanding, though more directed towards political *institutions* than practice. This perhaps imparts a more utopian, or theoretical, flavour to the text. Brobdingnag shows what England might conceivably be if certain fundamental reforms are undertaken; reforms that the King makes a comprehensive job of pointing out. They are wide-ranging, certainly, amounting to a recharging of the spirit of Englishness. Gulliver's adventures in Brobdingnag are an appeal to the average Englishman to reconsider the grounds of his patriotism. Brobdingnag is no perfect society, but with a King who rules in harmonious co-operation with his people and has no policy of aggressive international expansion, it is a model for the society that England might hope to be.

On, then, to Laputa.

3. A Voyage to Laputa, Balnibarbi, Glubbdubdrib, Luggnagg and Japan

Book 3 is a very different kind of reading experience from that of the other two books. Perhaps a few words of introduction are necessary before you set out on a voyage which will teach you a good deal about yourself as a reader. I have no wish to prejudice your 'set' towards the text, but it is fair to say that many readers find a good deal of difficulty with the third voyage. Here, for example, is the opinion of an experienced Swiftian:

> In comparison with the rest of *Gulliver's Travels* A Voyage to Laputa
> [etc] is of marked inferiority; this was the judgement of the first
> readers of the satire and it has never been reversed. The reasons for
> this inferiority are not far to seek. Part III was the last section of the
> book to be written . . . when he came to it, Swift had already finished
> part IV, which is the intellectual and emotional climax of the satire; a
> let-down was inevitable. Furthermore, Swift had worked out no
> unifying scheme for this voyage; he was in a mood of artistic relax-
> ation, content to make of this portion of the work a catch-all for satiric
> fragments for which no place had been found in the other three parts.[1]

**Without yet knowing the text, can you discern what assumptions
underlie this value-judgement, and what is your opinion of them?**

DISCUSSION

Quintana links the chronology of composition with literary merit, to suggest that Swift was on holiday when he wrote this part of the work. That is biographically very dubious, and lousy criticism. What does 'he was in a mood of artistic relaxation' *mean*? We might just as well say that what he wrote last was liable to be best because the overall shape of the work would now be clear. Quintana also suggests that this part was a rubbish-bin for all sorts of odds and ends, and that it therefore lacks a 'unifying scheme'. The satire, he complains, is too specific, far too densely rooted in quotidian reality, to have lasting literary merit. On these assumptions, it seems that 'great' satire works on a level of generality that transcends the specific material conditions of its production and speaks directly to us across the centuries. Handling 'universal' themes, it imposes 'unity' or 'organic unity' on its subject-matter by virtue of arranging its details round these eternal verities. This is an argument often applied to establish that great literature is that which endures. Satire does not do well on it, and eighteenth-century satire in particular suffers from the application of these criteria. As we have already seen, satire is often conveyed by the operation of the rhetorical device that we call 'irony'. Often, to gauge precisely the effect of irony, we need to know what the implied author *intended* to be ironic about. We need to renounce the explicit intentions behind the language and reconstruct the implicit intentions of the implied author. Unsurprisingly, these will bear some relation to the intentions of the actual, historical author, and so it becomes imperative, to understand satire, to *know something* about the actual historical context. Satire is, in my view, more deeply rooted in its contemporary background than other literary modes, owing to the intentionalist dimension of ironic meaning. I propose that we approach the text open-mindedly, keeping the issues of 'unity' and 'transcendent' versus 'specific' forms of satire in the background until we reach the end of the voyage.

Read the first two chapters, comparing them with those of Books 1 and 2. How do you react to the unidentified flying object encountered in chapter 1? With chapter 2, try to establish the general drift of the satire – what is being satirized and from what point of view? Specifically, why are mathematics and music identified as particular objects of satire? Please look carefully at the passage beginning chapter 2, down to 'kennel' (pp. 200–1), and consider the nature of the 'intense speculations' that preoccupy the people. Why are such 'speculations' being satirized? Give some thought to possible meanings of the word 'speculation' as we previously did with

'pride'. Look also at the passage, pages 207–8, beginning 'the women of the island . . . heard of since'.

DISCUSSION

In Lilliput, a storm; in Brobdingnag, a storm but with the added complication that Gulliver's shipmates leave him to his fate; and now, Gulliver has been marooned for defending Christian values. He is the victim of moral, rather than of natural evil. What did you make of the landscape that Gulliver encounters? Is it 'mere description', or does it also signify, i.e. function as a complex of signs which encode a meaning for the reader? In Lilliput and Brobdingnag, Gulliver had no difficulty getting onto the landmass. By comparison, this is a very *inconvenient* environment, rather than a dangerous one; and with the description of its rocky barrenness, its 'tufts of grass, and sweet-smelling herbs', its turf that serves as bedding and fuel, it seems oddly familiar:

> Around our house there stood little hills all tilled and tame. Yellow flame-blossoms of the whin lit bonfires all over the landscape; the whin was as persistent and as fertile as sin and disease. The sunny side of the hills was good soil and boasted some tall thorn trees, but the black side facing the north was crabbed and poverty-stricken and grew only stunted blackthorns and sorrel plants.

So the contemporary poet Patrick Kavanagh has described County Monaghan in Ireland, but maybe this is to domesticate Laputan scenery too far.[2] At any rate, its desolation strikes Gulliver with despair (as we know Ireland's uncultivated scenery frequently did Swift).

Shortly, however, the naturalness of this landscape is to be completely effaced by a very unnatural eclipse. As the Unidentified Flying Object darkens the sky, it may strike the reader that the fictional *mode* is about to change. In previous voyages, the fiction worked by means of an adjustment to the laws of human physiology, enabling people to be six times larger or smaller than we know them to be. Now, however, the focus is on a gravity-defying technological innovation which, at the time of writing, would defy all known laws of physics and mechanics. A different species of improbability is at work here, and it does, in my view, shift the fiction into the futuristic, or sci-fi mode.[3] Futuristic fiction or prototypical science-fiction may prove more difficult for the reader to find a bearing on since s/he cannot tell how radically a new technology might alter human behaviour. We cannot know what may be possible in this environment and must feel uneasy about the fictional 'contract' that the implied author is making with us.

**Look now at the passage I selected on pages 200–1. Establish first the
general field of the satire and then see if you can get the precise target
more directly in your sights.**

DISCUSSION

The key sentence is 'the minds of these people are so taken up with
intense speculations, that they neither can speak, nor attend to the
discourses of others, without being roused by some external taction
upon the organs of speech and hearing'. A normal human activity
(what was believed in Swift's time to be a *defining* human activity),
conversation or discussion by means of speech, seems unnaturally
difficult to perform in this soceity. Thought ('speculation') does not
seem to issue in its natural physiological manifestation – speech; and
the sensory functions of hearing and (latterly) seeing are performed
by intermediaries. I would like you to consult the *Oxford English
Dictionary* entry for the word 'speculation'. Can you apply the
information gained to this passage? I hope you can. Initially, this
word referred to the faculty of sight; but by way of 'observation of
the heavens', it came to have the more introverted sense of 'contem-
plation of a profound, far-reaching, or subtle character; abstract or
hypothetical reasoning on subjects of a deep, abstruse or conjectural
nature'. Judging by the *OED*'s examples, the word was acquiring
pejorative connations – '*mere* speculation' – in our period. It was
coming to mean impractical, inapplicable theorizing that does not
necessarily meet the hard facts of a case. Maybe the semantic
mutation of this word gives us the basis of the satire. These people,
with one eye fixed on the heavenly bodies and the other narcissisti-
cally focused on their own innermost beings, decorated with the
trappings of astronomy and music, walk their precarious island like
somnambulists. They speculate, but like Banquo's ghost, there is no
speculation in their eyes. Their frail bodies are inept machines, whose
ghostly pilots have better things to think about, and only menial
functionaries stand between them and the posts and 'kennels' (*not*
dog kennels – look it up!) that are the very hard facts of their
existence. To my mind, this is a very impressive, very economical
passage that concretely symbolizes a fundamental division in
eighteenth-century thought (a division that is still current) between
the practical and the theoretical intelligence. Other binarisms are
also implicated: body and mind, thought and action. Gulliver is here
observing a divided, schizophrenic society from his common-sense
or 'natural' standpoint.

   As we read on, we find that Laputan interests centre on music,
mathematics and astronomy. I asked you to speculate(!) on why this

group of disciplines should be selected for satirical attention. Obviously, any society obsessive enough to carry its curriculum into its clothing design and its culinary arts deserves to be laughed at. In general terms, this is a society that values theory over practice, and seems to have no place for recreation. But why *this* particular curriculum? The answer may lie in the knowledge that 'the people of their island had their ears adapted to hear the music of the spheres' (p. 204). As the *Oxford Companion to Music* informs me, an ancient Greek theory assumed that there was a correlation between the direct numerical proportions of musical consonance and the proportions that govern the ordering of the universe. Each planet emitted a musical sound that harmonized with all the others and was audible, though unrecognized, on earth. This theory neatly embraces geometry, astronomy and music in an ideal alliance. Influential up to the Renaissance, the idea, beautiful though it sounds, had become in the eighteenth century an intimation of insanity. As their belief in this ancient theory hints, Laputan education is benighted and backward-looking, recalling as it does the medieval division of secular knowledge into the elementary *Trivium* (grammar, rhetoric and dialectic) and the advanced *Quadrivium* (arithmetic, geometry, astronomy and music). The Laputans teach the *Quadrivium*, more or less, and have not caught up with more recent educational advances, especially those that, in the late sixteenth century, separated the *art* of music from its scientific or mathematical theory. Writing in 1740 a treatise called *The Art of Musick*, John Frederick Lampe makes the point clearly:

> The original Cause of the Mistakes, that have been made by some of the most learned among the Ancients in *Musick* was, that they took their first Principles from the *Mathematicks*, and by endeavouring to make *Musick* subservient to Numbers and Lines, and by calculating Proportions, have done themselves infinite Prejudice . . . Had it been duly considered, that the Knowledge of the Nature of all Sound depends upon the Sense of Hearing, they would have easily found, that *Musick* is not confined to *Mathematicks*, nor would they have taken so much Pains, to settle a System upon such Principles, which (*were they strictly followed*) would deprive us of the greatest Part of the *Beauties* of Musick.   pp. 2–3

Lampe encourages us to *listen* to music. Use your ears and forget about counting beats. Yet this is precisely what the Laputans, trapped in their sense-less mental prisons, are unable to do, which is presumably why their own music is a cacophony. You will find other examples of this Laputan habit. Turn, for example, to pages 204–6 and consider how these details about Laputan tradesmen illustrate the valorizing of theory over practice. As an academic, I have many times been accused of being some kind of Laputan, stuck in his (yawn) ivory tower. Swift's satire here, despite what adverse criticism of Book 3 suggests, is not especially esoteric or difficult to apply.

Are there any other features of Laputan society that are singled out for criticism? Make a note of any other satiric targets that come to your notice in this chapter. You might consider the religious and political implications of their beliefs in 'judicial astrology', expounded on pages 206–7.

DISCUSSION

(1) Despite the seeming theoretical sophistication that these people possess, they live in a medieval state of terror over the imminent extinction of the earth. This is of a piece with their 'great faith in judicial astrology'. Astronomy, the science of the cosmos, does very little for them other than exposing them to anxieties 'which very little affect the rest of mortals'. For the present-day reader, living in the nuclear era, there is nothing ridiculous about the idea of the imminent extinction of the earth, but nuclear power is, we hope, under our control. At all events, we can't live our lives effectively if we are continually feeling the prospect of extinction along the pulses. Swift's point here is that it is a form of *pride* to allow our lives to be ruled by cosmic phenomena over which we have absolutely no control. What is called for is, not exactly a fatalistic attitude, but a pragmatic one that allows us to get on with the business of living. Recalling John Gay's flea and the critique of 'anthropocentrism' – that is, the belief that mankind is the central element in the creation – the Laputans are extremely presumptuous. To Swift, there is something unpleasantly self-important in the quasi-millenarian fear of the end of the world. Curiously blending science and superstition, then, the Laputans resemble a privileged priest-class of astronomer-prophets, and this brings me on to my second point.

(2) There are hints that these magi in intellectual semi-retirement determine the social priorities of their community, while those who do the real work, the flappers, remain an exploited under-class. I think of the ancient Druids, the learned priest-magicians who were said to hold great power in Britain prior to Romanization and whose favourite study was astrological astronomy.[4] In some eighteenth-century traditions, they are said to have worn the heavenly bodies embroidered on their clothes. Any very positive identification of this sort would be too narrow, but I think we need to get at the sense of a science that is ultimately put at the disposal of divination or sooth-saying, and that then becomes a power-base for repression of others.

Already we can sense in the Island's dealings with the mainland city of Lagado (p. 205), an undesirably 'elevated' relationship, and this the next chapter will develop. To sum up, Laputa is a community of high-caste theoreticians whose interests in music and mathematics may seem modern, but on examination prove to be medieval or even more ancient. Even the flappers with their portable bean-bags seem like court-jesters, King Lear's Fools continually bringing their social superiors to their senses.

Look closely now at the passage on pages 207–8 about Laputan women. Is this an anti-feminist ridicule of women with low morals, or does it ridicule Laputan males?

DISCUSSION

The usual early eighteenth-century view of marital fidelity comes down to us typically in comedies. A cuckolded husband was often a figure of fun. He has proved unequal to the task of *containing* his wife – the woman who is in law virtually his property. She has acted autonomously in forming a liaison with another man. Almost as if a man's dining table were to get up on its legs and walk out of the room, the husband's chattel has developed a mind and body of its own. Cuckold's horns, the mark of the beast, are the fitting symbol for a husband thus distinguished.

Norms like these do operate behind this passage in *Gulliver's Travels*, which develops rather like a bedroom farce. In a play called *Three Hours After Marriage* (1717), written jointly by three close friends of Swift's (Gay, Pope and Arbuthnot), an Egyptologist and museum-curator called Dr Fossile has just married the worldly-wise and very young Mrs Townley. On the very afternoon of his nuptials, before consummation, he is almost cuckolded by the rakish actors Plotwell and Underplot, who gain access to his inner sanctum disguised as two museum exhibits, an alligator and a mummy. The motif of the 'virtuoso', the obsessive collector pitted against the man and woman of the world is mapped onto the timeless comic theme of the January/May romance. Fossile prefers rust to lust and, as his name suggests, *he* is the real museum piece. In the passage we are examining, the womens' 'vivacity' contrasts with the mens' 'specu-lation' – life versus lifelessness. As a bedroom farce, however, it lacks excitement because Laputan husbands are not really protecting their investments: 'the vexation is, that they act with too much ease and security' (p. 207). Once again, then, the irony cuts both ways, biting deeply into the clichés that define the co-ordinates of the eighteenth-century sex war.

To read the story of the 'great Court lady' that follows on page 208, I think we have to understand a distinction that was commonly made by literary critics and theorists in Swift's time, between *particular* and *general* satire. 'Particular' satire was satire that actually named names and therefore was impossible to miss, whereas 'general' satire confined itself to less identifiable targets, criticizing perennial human themes. Satirists normally *claimed* to be writing general satire, which was critically respectable.[5] In fact, however, any satirist worth his salt was able to combine both, by skilfully enabling the possibility of identification while avoiding certainty. Alexander Pope was the great master of this evasive hybrid. I wonder if, in the story of the 'great Court lady', as Gulliver says, 'an European or English story', you detect, as I do, the pressure of *particular* satire behind the text? I just can't believe that contemporary readers were not expected to speculate on the identities of this unhappy triangle. On a general level, the passage makes its timeless point about the perversity of woman; except that this shopsoiled cliché is invigorated here by the sense that *this* woman prefers actual bodily harm to the gracious neglect of her husband. Anything to be on the side of *life*. For eighteenth-century readers, there was also the great pleasure of the question 'who are these people?' At the risk of excessive scholarship, I shall pursue this question further. I'm a little self-conscious in the presence of the Laputans, but I hope to demonstrate something about how eighteenth-century satire functions, as well as something about how scholarship functions.

Mention of the 'prime Minister' in 1726 would alert readers to the affairs of the illustrious Sir Robert Walpole; specifically, his talked-about affair with Molly Skerrett by whom he had an illegitimate daughter in 1725. Even though the facts don't fit Walpole's case precisely, there is enough here to whet the contemporary appetite for scandalous 'application'. More precisely apposite was the case of John Dormer, Esq., his wife Diana and the footman Thomas Jones.[6] This notorious divorce was written up in the scandal-monger Edmund Curll's 1723 printing of *Cases of Divorce for Several Causes*. His juicy morsel is worth quoting because of the way it reproduces so clearly the period stereotypes of class and gender:

> There is not the least Room for any Thing like a favourable Construction of her Proceedure, whether we consider her Ingratitude to so good a Husband as Mr. *Dormer*, who rais'd her from a very low Degree of Life, to the Dignity of a Woman of condition; or the scandalous Manner of her Prostitution to one of her most inferior Servants, from whom she met with a Treatment suitable to so detestable a Familiarity between a Footman, that dar'd to commit the vilest Acts of Lewdness with his Mistress, even while he wore her Husband's Livery on his Back . . .

It should be apparent that the satire in this passage of *Gulliver's Travels* sets up a complicated interplay with the stereotypes on chastity and lewdness nakedly expressed in the above-quoted passage from the 'unspeakable Curll'. It also functions to enable individual identifications, and even political allusions, while generalizing out towards cultural norms of human sexual behaviour.

Chapters 3–5

I have tried, as a rule, to avoid overloading the reader with references to secondary material on *Gulliver's Travels* in the course of this discussion, preferring to emphasize the text itself. There is, however, a scholar whose work seems to me to be especially illuminating for the next three chapters. Marjorie Nicolson's important essay 'The Scientific Background of Swift's *Voyage to Laputa*' was published in 1937 and it was deeply influential on subsequent opinions of Book 3.[7] Previously considered a 'circular file' for satirical material that he couldn't place elsewhere in the book, the voyage to Laputa was shown by Nicolson to allude systematically to experiments actually conducted under the aegis of the Royal Society, formed in 1660 to 'scrutinize the whole of Nature and to investigate its activity and powers by means of observations and experiments', as the first Secretary, Henry Oldenburg, expressed it. These experiments were recorded in the Society's reports, *The Philosophical Transactions*; and from these records, Nicolson culled many experiments no less strange than those 'invented' by Swift in chapters 4 and 5. The work of the Royal Society is certainly one source of Swift's inspiration and one major target of his satire. Knowing this does not, in itself, make it any more successful or enjoyable to the modern reader, but it does disarm the criticism that the material of this voyage is bizarre or pointless or sheer fantasy. Understanding is the mother of appreciation and if we can come to understand why Swift should find a target in recent science, we will be preparing the way for a higher estimation of the voyage's artistic achievement.

Read the three chapters now and regarding chapter 3, jot down your sense of what seems to be wrong with the relationship between Laputa and Balnibarbi. Also, you may want to pick up again the question of allegory. If you do, please consult note 8 to this chapter, where some further reading suggestions are made. I shall proceed meanwhile with the relationship between Laputa and Balnibarbi.

DISCUSSION

Of the description of the Flying Island, I need only say that it is very close in form to the descriptions of far-away places with strange-sounding names that correspondents were sending regularly to the Royal Society secretariat. Sir Hans Sloane's *History of Jamaica*, completed in 1725, would offer a close enough parallel to Gulliver's factual, unadorned style of reportage. There was already an extensive literature on the effects of magnetism, many works including diagrams, so again, Swift would have found sources readily at hand.

Regarding the politics of the situation, I first notice the sinister symbiosis that exists between mainland and island (colony and motherland?): 'this island cannot move beyond the extent of the dominions below, nor can it rise above the height of four miles' (p. 212). Kept under aerial surveillance by the astronomers (Ministers?) who do the Monarch's bidding, the mainland's destiny appears to be unhealthily connected to that of the island. Like Gulliver and the Lilliputians, Balnibarbi and Lagado are locked into a fundamental hostility that could ultimately result in mutually assured destruction. Enslaving or destroying Balnibarbi are options taken off the political agenda only by the vested interests of Laputan absentee landlords who 'maintain their estates below on the continent'. Grievous nuisance, like withholding the sun and the rain (repressive trade laws?) and pelting them with stones (limited military action?), is as far as they can afford to go. In passing, I would point out that despite the seeming unwordliness of the Laputans, they do seem to have an iron grip on the political realities of their relationship with the Balnibarbians. Again, I suspect that the element of inconsistency in this would not be tolerable if *Gulliver's Travels* were perceived as a novel. If full weight is given to the satiric intentions, however, points can be made about unreciprocal and repressive political arrangements as well as about excessive theorizing and unpracticality, even at some cost to probability.

Proceed now to chapter 4. Give some thought to two questions:

(1) How far is Gulliver's character developing at this stage in the book?
(2) What function does the introduction of the character of Lord Munodi serve? (Examine carefully pp. 219–21.)

DISCUSSION

(1) Not very far, I fear! In this voyage up until now, Gulliver seems to operate as little more than a recording device, observing the

practices of the Laputans and the Balnibarbians with critical dis-
favour: 'I have not seen a more clumsy, awkward, and unhandy
people, nor so slow and perplexed in their conceptions upon all other
subjects' (p. 205). By contrast to the previous voyages, he is not in
any personal danger, so the narrative does not exploit the kind of
suspense that promotes reader-identification and increases interest
in a character's resources. For the most part, too, the implied author
is *firmly behind* him on this voyage so far, broadly endorsing his
verdicts. It may be that for a character to 'develop', as we say, some
independence from the value-system of the implied author must be
gained, or the character comes close to being an authorial mouthpiece. On the infrequent occasions when Gulliver's own views take
on a higher profile, such as when he 'venture(s) to offer' a conjecture
on the etymology of the name 'Laputa' (pp. 203–4 – a name,
incidentally, that Spanish speakers would immediately recognize as
meaning 'whore'), he seems to develop this scholarly facet to his
character not in any convincing way, but so that the implied author
can have a joke at the expense of earnest editorial labours. Once
again, though, I repeat that this is a more acute problem if we
continue to regard *Gulliver's Travels* as a novel. As a satiric device,
Gulliver goes on being quietly subversive. He calls into question the
value-system of a society whose aristocrats disparage him and banish
him to the 'downstairs' world of 'women, tradesmen, *flappers*, and
Court-pages' (p. 217).

(2) Lord Munodi is a broker in the alliance between narrator and
implied author that characterizes this voyage, in contrast to the
oppositional relationship in Brobdingnag. In other words, he is what
in the drama might be called a *raissoneur* figure, who directs the
reader's judgement and confirms the reader in the conclusions s/he is
independently drawing. Several attempts have been made to identify
Munodi precisely and to find an exact equivalent in contemporary
politics for the fiasco of his failed mill. Important figures in Swift's
life – Sir William Temple, Lord Bolingbroke, Lord Harley and
Viscount Midleton – have been proposed as the originals of this
portrait. I suggest that the ease with which it is possible to produce
these identifications makes the enterprise suspect. Munodi is an
exemplary character, an image of the desirable authority-
relationship between landlord and estate, owner and tenant, that
is breached in Laputan society as a whole. As in Lilliput and
Brobdingnag, there *are* references to immediate contemporary realities encoded here. Throughout this book, Swift's remote nations are
not entirely countries of the mind. They proceed from a searching
analysis of his own society and at times are a clarion call to specific

social action. I began this phase of the discussion with a suggestion
that Balnibarbian terrain might echo Irish countryside; in note 8, I've
asked interested readers to do a little research into the Wood's
Halfpence affair. It should be clear that I think there is *some* analogy
between Laputa/Balnibarbi and England/Ireland operating here, but
again, I would resist any reduction of the text only to that.

Do you detect, on the journey to Munodi's estate, pages 219–
20, any echoes of the voyage to Brobdingnag, especially in the
reference to the absence of 'one ear of corn or blade of grass'? This
echoes the King of Brobdingnag's memorable definition of the true
patriot-politician as one who 'could make two ears of corn, or two
blades of grass to grow upon a spot of ground where only one grew
before' (p. 176). Munodi is such a man. His estate is an oasis in a
desert of poverty and disorder. Eighteenth-century readers would
have been especially sensitive to the paragraph (p. 218) that shows
this confusion to obtain in town *and* countryside, because they
were brought up on literary modes (the 'pastoral' and the 'georgic')
that turned on *opposition* between the fallen city and the idealized
rustic retreat of the countryside, with its orderly images of produc-
tive labour and regenerative recreation. In Balnibarbi, both the
urban 'proletariat' and the agricultural peasantry are in a bad way.
Munodi's carefully-tended estate, testifying to the *presence*, not the
absence of the landlord, is the positive term in a satiric attack on the
displacement of traditional values. Unmistakably, Munodi is a
traditional landed aristocrat who has put his house in order, but is so
far out of tune with the times that pressure is forcing him to conform.
(Munodi's elegiac sadness, the tones in which he talks of having to
'throw down his houses in town and country, to rebuild them after
the present mode, destroy all his plantations' (p. 221) reminds me of
the Biblical prophet Jeremiah, whom the Lord set over nations and
over the kingdoms 'to root out, and to pull down, and to destroy, and
to throw down, to build, and plant' (*Jeremiah* 1.10).) Munodi's
house, 'built according to the best rules of ancient architecture', is an
extension of the moral excellences of its owner and is a standing
reproof – but for how much longer? – to 'modern usage'.

The Academy of Lagado (pp. 221–37)

The next two chapters are occupied by a description of the activities
taking place in the Academy of Lagado, so it is important that we
gain a clear understanding of what the Academy represents. For
readers coming fresh to *Gulliver's Travels* in the late twentieth-
century, the attack on science and technology that is mounted in this
section is difficult to fathom. Science and technology are so highly

regarded in our present-day culture, and the benefits of scientific
progress in terms of material prosperity seem so patent (whatever the
problems raised by ecological pollution), that it is initially hard to
imagine how Swift could have been so entirely on the losing side of
the argument. Reading this section is going to demand of you a
greater effort of the historical imagination than you have yet had to
make. The question to keep in mind is *why* does Gulliver's report on
the Academy of Lagado, based as it is in part on actual experiments
conducted under the auspices of the Royal Society, come down so
heavily against applied, empirical science? I want you to pause now
and ponder the question. I am supplying extracts from two recent
books (both of which are richly rewarding to read in full) that will
help to direct your thoughts:

(a) It is also clear that Baconianism [a method of scientific investigation based on close observation of the world, argued for by Sir
Francis Bacon] encouraged indiscriminate collecting of information relevant to no particular hypothesis. This was inevitable in
some subjects, such as the study of heat, where there was no
research tradition to draw on; it was encouraged by the new
exactitude of observation made possible by scientific instruments
which justified experiment almost for its own sake. But Baconianism also encouraged random collecting in subjects where it was
unconstructive, enabling those lacking in imagination to make a
virtue of their abstention from philosophical speculation. The
charter for such activity was provided by Bacon's idea of a
'natural history', the store of data from which hypotheses were to
be inductively derived, [i.e. derived by observing regular conjunc-
tions of cause and effect between related phenomena] perhaps his
most significant methodological legacy to seventeenth-century
science.

The Academy is first introduced to us by Munodi in the context of a
distinction between what is *ancient* and what is *modern*. In Swift's
period, there was a vigorous quarrel conducted between those who
supported the claims of 'ancient' learning and those who felt that
'modern' scholars and scientists had progressed beyond the earlier
sages of classical Greece and Rome. In this extract from Joseph M.
Levine the distinction is explained:

(b) The contest [between the 'ancients' and the 'moderns'] was
between two antithetical forms of culture or education . . . On the
one hand, there was the notion that the imitation of classical
literature, especially the Latin works of the Augustan age, was the
sole means to success in life and art; this was the conviction of the
'ancients'. The classics were the best; the sum of human achievement lay in the past. But this carried with it from the first an
indifference, sometimes even a hostility, to classical philosophy

> and science . . . On the other hand, the revival of antiquity had
> from the first meant also the restoration of classical culture in a
> much wider sense, and this carried with it [a] 'modern' con-
> sequence . . . It meant . . . the recovery of ancient thought as a
> whole, including science and philosophy, and hence one of the
> foundations on which was built the impressive new philosophical
> speculation of seventeenth-century Europe.[9]

**With these passages in mind, read through chapter 5 and try to
establish *why* the projects described are singled out as absurd and
useless.**

DISCUSSION

Munodi, a traditionalist and an 'ancient', introduces the Academy in
the context of the 'modern' idealism that motivated its establishment. His statement emphasizes the 'newness', the novelty of the
projects being pursued. Notice the slippage from conceivably useful
research to plans that pervert the course of nature ('All the fruits of
the earth shall come to maturity at whatever season we think fit to
choose').

Some additional information is perhaps useful at this point.
Lying behind the academy is the seventeenth-century lawyer Francis
Bacon's great philosophical system, the *Instauratio magna*. One
small part of this was Bacon's utopian fragment *New Atlantis*, first
published in 1627. Dominating the community of New Atlantis is an
institution called Salomon's House, a research foundation staffed by
enormously privileged Fellows and dedicated to 'the knowledge of
Causes, and secret motions of things; and the enlarging of the bounds
of Human Empire, to the effecting of all things possible'. It includes
mines, towers, zoological gardens, botanical gardens, lakes, fur-
naces, chambers for optical and acoustical experiments, engineering
plants and so on, making available masses of information for
other scholars to collect, sift, frame hypotheses and develop more
advanced experiments. The Academy of Lagado is an *inverse*
Salomon's House, wherein the Baconian empiricist impulse has led
to experiments that seem to have more in common with alchemy
than with anything that we might consider truly scientific.[10] The 'silks
from spiders' project is of particular significance, because spiders
function in Swift's writings as peculiarly charged symbols. Spiders
spin their webs out of their own entrails. They are therefore fitting
symbols for those 'moderns' who are also building without foundations. Readers who wish to pursue this symbolism further in Swift
are directed at this point to note 11. Dismissing all the accumulated
wisdom of the ancients, throwing away like old lumber the furniture

of the mind, these experimenters try to create the world anew every day. You may have noticed the self-consuming tendency of the experiments, how some of them (like the cure for colic) seem to involve little more than re-cycling their own foul ingredients. When we move to the section of the Academy given over to 'the projectors in speculative learning', the point becomes even clearer.

I want you to examine carefully the speculative projects detailed on pages 227–31. Consider these questions:

(1) In what way is the object of satirical attack similar to or different from that in Laputa?
(2) Why should the relationship between *words* and *things* be singled out for particular consideration?

DISCUSSION

(1) It is different in that these 'projectors' can't be accused of living in the 'airy region' of Laputan theoretical speculation. 'Speculation' releases yet another of its meanings in this context – investment undertaken for financial gain. These projectors are not, after all, the responsible altruists of Bacon's Salomon's House, putting whatever findings they deem truly socially beneficial in the hands of the state. They endure their foetid environment in the hope of eventual financial return. Laputan speculation is commercially disinterested, if also a weapon of social hegemony.[12] In the Academy of Lagado, a manifestation of early eighteenth-century capitalism known as the 'projecting spirit' and exemplified in the soda-fountain of ideas that spurted from the pen of a writer like Daniel Defoe, is satirized. Propagating 'naked sheep' is vividly symbolic of what Swift saw as the bankruptcy of such bids for fame and fortune. So that what Laputan theory and Lagadan praxis have in common is that they are both being judged by a criterion of *social usefulness*. They are no earthly *use*. They don't make two ears of corn grow where one grew before. Lord Munodi does that, using entirely traditional methods. What is *your* view about this? Be thinking about where you stand on this issue, because I'll take up the question at the end of the chapter.

(2) We have already raised the subject of words and objects in connection with political allegory in Lilliput, in saying that allegory presumes a certain way in which words are held to signify – to have meaning. We have also talked about Swift's prose style being 'plain', that is, eschewing figurative elaboration. The relation of *res et verba*, words and things, was a fundamental issue addressed by rhetoricians since time immemorial, and by Swift's time, it had grown in

importance due to the attention paid to it by the two major philosophers of language, John Locke and George Berkeley. Their views were crucially different in that for Locke, most words are signs for ideas existing in the speaker's mind, which, in turn, were mental representations of real objects:

> *Words in their primary or immediate Signification, stand for nothing, but the* ideas *in the Mind of him that uses them* . . . That then which Words are the Marks of, are the *Ideas* of the Speaker.
> *Essay Concerning Human Understanding*, 3.2.2

For Berkeley, however, there were no 'real objects' existing outside the realm of ideas, so that there can be no distinction between ideas and their 'contents'. For Locke, the word 'house', is an arbitrarily assigned term designating the idea 'house', which is a mental representation of the thing that is a house. For Berkeley, houses don't exist apart from our ideas of them; the idea *is* the house, and so words are signs of ideas which in turn are signs of other ideas . . . and you can never break out of the verbal circle. Meanings are determined not by correspondence to outside reality, but by the overall context in which the signs occur.[13] Philosophical questions about how language makes application to the world are, very broadly speaking, the background to this section of *Gulliver's Travels*. An enduring preoccupation of Swift's writing is the attempt to find an acceptable relationship between words and their objects. What terrified and excited him was the spectre of words coming adrift from their moorings in reality and setting up an independent realm of pure language. In a letter to the Earl of Oxford later published as *A Proposal for Correcting, Improving and Ascertaining the English Tongue*, Swift had suggested the foundation of an English Academy on the model of the Académie française, which would arrest what he took to be the gradual corruption of the language. Equally, however, Swift was appalled by the thought of an entirely rational language, computer-speak where words and their objects had an inhuman fixity of equivalence. At times, Swift questions any capacity words have to actually apply to the world:

> Will any man say that if the words *whoring, drinking, cheating, lying, stealing*, were by act of parliament ejected out of the English tongue and dictionaries, we should all awake next morning chaste and temperate, honest and just, and lovers of truth?

he asks, in the *Argument [against] the Abolishing of Christianity in England*.

I suggest you look again in detail at the two schemes being undertaken by 'the projectors in speculative learning' outlined on pages

227–31; the project for writing books 'without the least assistance from genius or study' (p. 227), and the 'scheme for entirely abolishing all words whatsoever'. Can you determine where the satiric focus is, and how the irony is working? To assist you, I will supply a statement on prose style made in 1667 by Thomas Sprat, the first historian of the Royal Society. How do you think Sprat's ideal prose style measures up to the 'plain style' of Swift?

> [The Royal Society] have, therefore been most rigorous in putting in execution, the only *Remedy*, that can be found for this *extravagance*: [ornateness of style] and that has been, a constant Resolution; to reject all the amplifications, digressions and swellings of style: to return back to primitive purity, and shortness, when men deliver'd so many *things*, almost in an equal number of *words*.

DISCUSSION

Regarding the first scheme, the focus is not on linguistic theory, but on the conditions of book production. Books are physical objects and they can be reduced to a set of physical marks on paper. Eighteenth-century satire often stressed the secondary functions of cheap prints as lavatory paper and pie-dish lining. Margaret Spufford reminds us that this satire has a very material basis in the need for lavatory paper in the pre-Andrex era:

> We know this was so amongst the gentry, if Sir William Cornwallis is in any way typical. He kept 'pamphlets and lying-stories and two-penny poets' in his privy, to be read there, and then used. Although there is no evidence from further down the social scale, the need must have been just as great. If we admit as a witness the scurrilous song collected by Anthony Wood which begins 'Bum-Fodder or Wast-Paper proper to wipe the Nation's Rump with, or your own', we know that paper was pressed into general service in this way. This remained the doom of cheap print as late as the 1920s.[14]

Here, then, Gulliver is recording a method of book production that is truly the product of artificial intelligence. Cutting out the long gestation-period of independent study, and the writer's genius, this 'professor' creates books that can be reduced without residue to the paper they are printed on. Mere empty verbiage, collections of broken sentences, they stand for the pointless lucubrations of the 'modern' professional hack-writer.

The apologists for 'plain style' such as Sprat, in their compulsion to avoid metaphor and figure, sometimes seemed to Swift to wish to avoid *language* itself. Clearly, the ludicrous impracticality of carrying around sackfuls of objects is a *reductio ad absurdum* of Sprat's dream of plainness, of a language so transparent that its own

materiality never gets in the way of meaning. Here, Swift's irony
works in a similar way to the celebrated *A Modest Proposal*, in which
the proposer, using the tone of plain, honest common-sense, suggests
the monstrous plan of solving Ireland's problems of famine and
overpopulation by eating children. In the name of health, practical-
ity and convenience, a senseless proposal is mooted which seems to
gain the narrator's approval. Whatever the narrator says, however,
the implied author is as usual present to nudge us into endorsing the
action of the 'women in conjunction with the vulgar and illiterate' –
or at least partly endorsing it, for there is surely some residual
support from the implied narrator for Gulliver's ill-natured comment 'such constant irreconcilable enemies to science are the common people'. Yet again, the reader doesn't agree with the narrator,
but may not altogether accept what the implied narrator urges either.

We now move from the speculative part of the Academy to the
Faculty of 'political projectors', and are immediately introduced to a
group of professors that Gulliver pronounces to be 'wholly out of
their senses' (p. 232). **How do the political ideas expressed in the
opening paragraph relate to those of the King of Brobdingnag and
what view are we invited to take of them?**

DISCUSSION

Most readers will detect the similarity between the principles of
government to which the King of Brobdingnag is wedded, and the
aims that these professors in the Academy are trying to promote. In
Brobdingnag, however, these were worthy aims, deserving emulation. Why are they now proofs of insanity? Gulliver's memory-span
certainly seems shorter than that of a normally competent fictional
character. Until now, all of the projects that have been reported have
been clearly judged by the criterion of *utility* and found wanting.
Gulliver thinks they are absurd; so does the implied author; so does
the reader. Yet in their absurdity, they do symbolize some of the
broad intellectual tendencies of Swift's own age, as observed by a
hostile witness. *This* project is not 'extravagant and irrational': if
anything, it is *too* rational. What, exactly, is happening here?
Overtly, irony is being directed at political idealism or utopianism:
these aims are dismissed as 'wild impossible chimeras, that never
entered before into the heart of man to conceive'. Palpably, however,
they *have* entered at least into the King of Brobdingnag's heart. The
irony is therefore directed against any reader who is cynical enough
to *agree* with Gulliver here, and to relinquish any purchase on
idealistic political ends. Anyone who knows Cervantes's *Don*

Quixote might recognize a familiar satiric technique here. Don Quixote, the idealistic Knight-Errant, is satirized for his unworldly idealism which gets him into comic scrapes, but simultaneously the world is satirized for continually failing to live up to his idealism. Not for the first time, Swift has *unsettled* the reader, attacked the firm position from which s/he was evaluating the text. As we shall see, some critics have laid considerable stress on moments when the text wrong-foots the reader in this way, promoting them into a theory for reading Swift which has been called the 'reader-entrapment' theory. More of that later.

I now want to return to the question with which we began this study, and which has recurred at various times, that of 'realism'. I have said that *Gulliver's Travels* blurs the edges of the distinction between fact and fiction by creating the illusion that the narrator is a real person to whom the events narrated really occurred. Gulliver elaborately 'breaks the frame' of the narrative, steps out of the story to destroy any firm distinction between the world and the book; as, for example, when in the Court intrigue passage in Lilliput (p. 102) he exclaims of the informers Clustril and Drunlo 'I will name them, and let 'em make their best of it'. This implies that his actions may have consequences in the extra-fictional world, at the later time of narration. Or take for example the use of real personages like the map-maker Herman Moll, who did really exist. **I now want to examine this question of realism, or extra-fictionality, again – with reference to the Kingdom of Tribnia passage, pages 235–7. Do you think that this passage is 'realistic', or is it entirely a fictional invention? What relationship might exist between this episode and events that could conceivably occur in the world?**

DISCUSSION

At first, it seems as far-fetched as ever, and as unpleasant. All through chapter 6, a metaphor has been literalized. England, an unhealthy state, is a '*body* politic'. Various entirely physical cures have been proposed for what we know to be a figurative sickness. Medicines and surgery have been suggested to get the political patient back on his feet. It is a quintessentially Swiftian satiric procedure to treat a figure of speech, in this case the comparison of the state to an individual human body, as if it were a literal usage. To discover plots by examining the excrement of incriminated persons 'and from the colour, the odour, the taste(!), the consistence, the crudeness or maturity of digestion, form a judgement of their thoughts and designs' (pp. 235–6), is a suggestion that appears to continue the satire. It has the hallmarks of satirical exaggeration. In the tasteless scatological suggestion that government spies should eat their suspects' turds, in the very idea that non-material *thought* should be deducible from material ordure, this is unmistakably Swiftian. Surprisingly, however, the episode is probably the most unambiguously *topical* in the whole of *Gulliver's Travels*.[15] 'Tribnia' and 'Langden' are, of course, anagrams for Britain and England, and in 'Langden' in 1722–3, a close friend of Swift's, Bishop Francis Atterbury, had been tried for suspected involvement in a Jacobite plot and sent into exile. Two incriminating letters actually *were* retrieved from the Bishop's close-stool [a lavatory chair], though they were not the most crucial items of evidence.

Enter Swift. This passage is a satirical attack on the conduct of the Atterbury trial and the code-breaking activities of the Government. Many of the examples of deciphering have precise equivalents in the trial. Yet it is clearly a satirical hyperbole that pronounces 'the bulk of the people' to be 'discoverers, witnesses, informers, accusers, prosecutors, evidences, swearers' etc. – another of those open-ended catalogues that produce on the reader such a bleak, claustrophobic effect. And isn't there a paradox in the fact that to condemn this kind of allegorical reading, the reader actually has to *engage* in it? After all, the passage does not explicitly announce itself as being about the Atterbury trial. If we go back to the *facts* of the case, it is far from clear, despite the comic-satiric indignation here, that Swift's satirical attack on the Ministry was justified. Although the evidence against him was feeble, Atterbury *was* guilty; and no matter how self-parodic the evidence against him seemed, Atterbury's Jacobite correspondence was 'loaded down with codes and ciphers, pseudonyms and initials, to such an extent that it would achieve a kind of puerile, Tom-Sawyer quality, if we were not aware of the life-and-death reality which it reflects'.[16]

So where does this leave us? Gulliver poses in this passage as a worldly-wise political adept, who has a thing or two to teach even the professors of Lagado about incrimination of suspects. For the nonce, the implied author is not endorsing him, and as in the gunpowder incident in Brobdingnag, Gulliver is betraying his meanness of spirit. The reader knows the passage is ironic, because of the seeming hyperbole and the sheer lunacy of the interpretative procedures being recommended. On the other hand, the details are not arbitrarily chosen. They are themselves coded and to the knowing reader, will disclose the events of the Atterbury case. Just as other details in Book 3 reveal specific deviant tendencies in contemporary culture, this passage satirically condemns the abuse of political power, but does so by *employing* the very tactics it reviles. As a final ironic twist, history declares that the Atterbury affair was *not* a periodic manifestation of the 'Reds under the beds' mentality, but was an actual plot against Monarch and state. Nothing in Swift's satire reaches the heights of idiocy that the plot itself achieved. What price fact and fiction now? One of the most obviously fictional passages of *Gulliver's Travels* ripens into one of the most securely factual.

Chapters 7–8

From Lagado, Gulliver purposes to visit the island of Luggnagg, but is detained for a while on Glubbdubdrib, an island governed by magicians who are capable of summoning up figures from world history. Give some consideration to the following questions while reading the chapters:

(1) **What do we learn about history in these chapters? Look especially at the passage on pages 244–5 beginning 'Here I discovered . . .'**
(2) **Can you suggest why the six named 'worthies' on page 241 might have been selected for special mention?**
(3) **Can you establish any connection between this episode and the concerns of the earlier voyage to Laputa/Lagado?**

By way of orientation, I suggest you read the following passage from the second-century Greek satirist Lucian's hilarious imaginary voyage *A True History*. I quote from Thomas Brown's translation made in 1711. At this point, Lucian has reached the Isle of the Blest (or Fortunate Islands) where live the noble dead:

> I went to pay a visit to *Homer*, at a time when both of us were at leisure, and among other things made bold to ask him what Countryman he was, telling him, that this was a Controversie warmly debated with us. His answer was, that for his part he knew no more than the Man in the Moon: For some wou'd have him to be of *Chios*, others of *Smyrna*, and some again of *Colophon*. But to deliver his own opinion freely, he fansied himself to be a *Babylonian*, and that his Countrymen call'd him not Homer but *Tigranes*; but afterwards, when he became a Hostage among the *Greeks*, they changed his Name. Then I ask'd him whether he writ those Verses that were rejected, and he own'd them all to be written by himself, upon which I cou'd not but think with my self, how that foolish couple of Grammarians *Zenodotus* and *Aristarchus* [both later editors of Homer, who denied Homeric authorship for various writings] had banter'd the World with their impertinent Observations. After he had fully satisfied me as to this particular, I went on, and asked him for what reasons he had begun his Poem with the falling out between *Achilles* and *Agamemnon*. For no design at all, said he, but only the whim came into my Head. Then I begg'd him to inform me, whether, as some People pretended, he writ his *Odyseus* before his *Iliads*, and he told me no. I now found that the report of his being blind was without any Foundation.[17]

DISCUSSION

(1) Consider first *how* we learn about history. Just as we found in
Lilliput, beneath a seemingly smooth narrative surface a series of
jerky switches between modes, so now in Glubbdubdrib there has
been a switch from what I have classified as prototypical science
fiction to *Lucianic* satire. Lucian's fantasy voyage from which I have
given an excerpt above allows him, in its descent into the underworld
section, to take an irreverent and humorous look at the great heroes
of the past. Their reputations are cut down to manageable size. By
comparing their characteristically blunt and debunking replies to
questions with the traditions and mystifications that have grown up
around them, he is able to satirize the way in which knowledge about
the past is transmitted. Historiography, scholarly editions and com-
mentaries are shown to be propagating myths. No, Homer wasn't
Greek; and his name wasn't Homer! He did write various verses that
ponderous scholars have failed to attribute to him. Despite the reams
of clever criticism written about the opening of *The Iliad*, the idea
came to him quite by accident. And he wasn't blind. I think you will
see a very direct influence on the passage on page 242 about Homer
and Aristotle – Homer, whose 'eyes were the most quick and piercing
I ever beheld'. Swift, like Lucian, has his joke on the scholar-parasites
who 'so horribly misrepresented the meaning of those authors to
posterity'. Yet Lucianic satire here goes far beyond the puncturing of
scholarly labours or folk-tales about how Alexander the Great died
or how Hannibal cut his way through the Alps. Calling up the past as
witness to the present, Gulliver in Glubbdubdrib goes close to
suggesting that all of our knowledge of the past is a gigantic
conspiracy cooked up by 'prostitute writers, to ascribe the greatest
exploits in war to cowards, the wisest counsel to fools, sincerity to
flatterers, Roman virtue to betrayers of their country, piety to
atheists, chastity to sodomites, truth to informers' (p. 244). Humour
is left far behind as the discourse moves towards diatribe. Past events,
it seems, are normally the results of actions taken by vicious individuals: indeed, some monarchs are on record as saying that this
must be so because virtuous action is an administrative in-
convenience.[18] Historians are employed to dress up the past in the
robes of virtue and heroism; and this is especially true of genealogy
by means of which 'old illustrious families' legitimate their power
and social status. Again, the deeply subversive note of irony is
sounded when Gulliver refers to the titled and landed nobility. With
calculated understatement, Gulliver controls an anger that always
threatens to break its bounds in this section – 'I hope I may be
pardoned . . . their inferiors' (p. 246). Also noted is history's

capacity to *edit out* the actions of true patriots; and doubtless, the Roman patriot whose actions are detailed and who fails to find the career advancement he so richly deserved offers an invitation to contemporary readers to 'apply'. (They could do worse than look at Swift's own career.) In the end, Gulliver's privileged access to the past, his 'horse's mouth' experience of history, is appropriated to a theory about the progressive degeneration of the race, which was formerly documented in the story of the Brobdingnagian treatise (p. 178).

What is your opinion of the view of history promulgated here? I don't think it is very convincing. That there are 'events' perpetrated by vicious individuals and separately, a tribe of writers who conceal their true malice and conveniently forget the virtuous patriots, is pretty much of a nonsense. That is the kind of view that makes for scandalous or 'secret' history, just exactly the kind of hack product that is satirized on pages 244–5, but which, within seconds, Gulliver is actually *writing*: 'here I discovered the true causes of many great events . . .' (p. 245). And of course, the blanket indictment of past events and extreme scepticism about historical knowledge is incompatible with the degeneracy theory offered at the end, which seems to entail that people once were virtuous. The question arises whether Gulliver is the vehicle or the target of the satire here? What he learns in Glubbdubdrib is deeply subversive of established social hierarchies and power structures; nothing short of a dismantling of eighteenth-century ideology, since it dismantles the legitimacy of rank and succession. This is potential dynamite, except that the criticism seems too indiscriminate, too crude, and has a tendency to self-destruct.

(2) Some historical figures do, however, survive the generally scathing attack on modern history that is conducted in 3.8. For a moment, let me lead you up the garden path – to be precise, to Viscount Cobham's exquisite gardens at Stowe in Bucks., where, in 1726, the architect James Gibbs had erected a building surrounded by pedestals supporting busts of 'British worthies' sculpted by Michael Rysbrack. Those chosen included Queen Elizabeth, Shakespeare, Bacon, Milton, William III, Newton, Locke and Hampden; and it has been suggested that the building was inspired by a visit to Stowe that Pope, Swift and Gay made in 1726. By 1735, these 'worthies' had been moved to the so-called 'Elysian Fields', a part of the garden quite consciously designed to enact a Virgilian landscape of the blissful underworld. There was also a Temple of Ancient Virtue which contained four statues, of Homer, Epaminondas, Socrates and Lycurgus, all demonstrating a favourite

theme of the anti-Walpole opposition – 'Liberty threatened by Corruption'.[19] I see in the Sextumvirate selected by Gulliver an anticipation of the sacred landscape designed for Stowe. All of the six chosen share the qualities of virtuous poverty, benevolent friendship and a rational, tranquil attitude to death, as M. M. Kelsall argues in 'Iterum Houyhnhnm: Swift's Sextumvirate and the Horses'.[20] More significantly, though, they all resisted tyranny and corruption and were model patriots. They exemplify the strengths of the ancient world, from which modern life has so sadly declined. The Senate of Rome 'seemed to be an assembly of heroes and demigods; the [modern Parliament] a knot of pedlars, pickpockets, highwaymen and bullies' (p. 241). Just so, in Stowe, the Temple of Ancient Virtue was twinned by a Temple of Modern Virtue containing a headless statue.

(3) As to the connection between this episode and the earlier voyage to Laputa/Lagado, I concede at once that it is not tight. It is impossible to speak, here, of the 'necessity' with which parts are related to parts in, say, Aristotle's conception of tragedy. Nothing in Laputa/Lagado *necessitates* that Gulliver's next trip should be to a place where necromancy is possible. It should be obvious by now that even those parts of *Gulliver's Travels* in which critics habitually find unity (the first two voyages) are more aggregatory than 'organic', growing by means of the juxtaposition of parts in differing modes. This Lucianic section of *Gulliver's Travels* 3 is a different reading experience from what has preceded it. However, in the voyage as a whole, we have been concerned with knowledge. Theoretical 'speculation', empirical experiments designed to press knowledge into the service of technological innovation, technology bizarrely applied to authorship – these have been examined and have demonstrated the *uselessness* of recent intellectual endeavour. An individual's knowledge is dependent on memory; and the knowledge possessed by a nation is also dependent on the collective memory that we call history. If history is discredited, if what we 'know' about the past is a systematic falsification, then no secure basis exists for anything we can be said to know. By the time Gulliver leaves Glubbdubdrib, there is very little reason to retain much pride in recent scientific or philosophical advance, and there is grave uncertainty about the foundations of epistemology [theory of knowledge].

Chapters 9–11

I'm going to move on rapidly past the Court of the King of Luggnagg, though I recommend that you pause over pages 249–50 to analyse the shifts of tone that occur there. Clearly, this cameo portrait is of a monstrous parody of arbitrary power, a king who rules without any sense of the duties of his office. His way of disposing of unwanted aristocrats is so appalling that it is hard to see why it is also very funny. Perhaps you might give some thought to that question. I want to proceed directly to the episode of the Struldbruggs. In the *Life of Swift*, Dr Johnson expressed a low opinion of Book 3, which has gained subsequent currency, as we saw. He may have had the Struldbruggs in mind when he said that 'the greatest difficulty that occurs, in analysing [Swift's] character, is to discover by what depravity of intellect he took delight in revolving ideas from which almost every other mind shrinks with disgust. The ideas of pleasure, even when criminal, may solicit the imagination; but what has disease, deformity, and filth upon which the thoughts can be allured to dwell?' I'd like you to try to answer Johnson's question.

(1) **On what are our thoughts 'allured to dwell' in the account of the Struldbruggs?**

(2) **More specifically, give some attention to Gulliver's aspirations towards being the nation's historian on pages 254–5.**

DISCUSSION

(1) Woody Allen once joked, 'I don't want to gain immortality through my works. I want to gain it by *not dying*.' Desire for immortality is a very old literary theme and the ancient Greek story of Tithonus is a source of this episode. Here is the story of Tithonus as told by Swift's contemporary William King:

> *Aurora* . . . obtain'd from the *Parcae*, or Fates, that [Tithonus] might become immortal; but at the same time forgot to request that he might not grow old. Age and length of Time made him so decrepit, that he was forc'd as an Infant to be wrock'd to sleep in a Cradle; so that he thought it better to die, than to encounter with so many Troubles and Difficulties of Nature, but since he cou'd not obtain Death, he got *Aurora* to transform him to a Grasshopper.[21]

Aurora 'forgot to request' and in the space created by that oversight, the gods found room to punish Tithonus for his *hybris* in wishing to slough off the condition of mortality. Gulliver also overlooks the small difficulty that immortality is not equivalent to eternal youth, and although he isn't actually transformed into a grasshopper, he certainly ends up looking like a lemon! The longing for immortality is the ultimate form of pride because the fact of human senescence and mortality is a fundamental datum of our existence. To wish not to die is to wish to be inhuman, to be superhuman. Old age and its physical and mental unpleasantness (much more so then than now) was also a well-worn literary theme, ever since the Roman satirist Juvenal had graphically described it in his tenth satire.[22]

Staying on this episode for a little longer, it is worth paying attention to the way in which the discourse sets Gulliver up for satiric exposure in this chapter. Examine pages 252–5, and make some points on satiric method here. How is Gulliver's folly revealed to the reader?

To assist us in exploring this point, I want to introduce a fundamental distinction that is made by theorists of fiction. *Story* is distinguished from *discourse*. Each narrative has two parts, a certain content or chain of events (story) and the expression by means of which that content is communicated (discourse). We are able to give a plot-summary of, say, *Macbeth*, and in so doing, we are transmitting the story. ('Macbeth kills King Duncan . . .') But we are made aware of this story by means of a discourse that *deforms* it in certain ways, by manipulating time, by employing narrators, by changing locations and so on. 'Discourse', we might say, is how we are made aware of story.[23] An example of how this operates, relevant to *Gulliver's Travels*, is furnished by Samuel Johnson's *Rasselas* (1759). This delicate story begins with Prince Rasselas living in a utopia called the Happy Valley, where he is bored to distraction. Wishing to escape, he finds an inventor 'eminent for his knowledge of the mechanick powers', who is working on a flying machine. This inventor gives Rasselas a lengthy and rapturous disquisition on the possibility and rewards of flight – 'How must it amuse the pendent spectator to see the moving scene of land and ocean, cities and desarts! To survey with equal security the marts of trade, and the fields of battle' – with much more of the same. After swearing Rasselas to secrecy, the inventor is ready:

> In a year the wings were finished, and, on a morning appointed, the maker appeared furnished for flight on a little promontory: he waved his pinions a while to gather air, then leaped from his stand, and in an instant dropped into the lake. His wings, which were of no use in the air, sustained him in the water, and the prince drew him to land, half dead with terrour and vexation.

This is effective and funny because it has been so well prepared. Considerable discourse has been apportioned to the discussion *surrounding* the attempt, but the *flight itself* (which is, after all, the main story) is accorded half a sentence. Effectiveness inheres in the *ratio* of story to discourse; so that the discourse punishes the inventor for his pride by ducking him rapidly. A similar story: discourse ratio is responsible for setting Gulliver up in Luggnagg. First, some rapturously mealy-mouthed dialogue is invented for Gulliver – I say 'invented', because it isn't really in character for him to speak in such overblown exclamations as 'I cried out in a rapture; Happy nation where every child hath at least a chance of being immortal!' and so on (p. 253). Ignoring several warning signs which I think the reader probably catches (he rationalizes away the Struldbruggs' absence from court and doesn't construe the 'sort of smile which usually ariseth from pity to the ignorant'), Gulliver is easily persuaded into giving his views on the benefits of immortality. Like the inventor in *Rasselas*, he is being manoeuvred onto the top of a high cliff and will be kicked off it when the truth about the Struldbruggs comes out. Reading this for the first time, at what point did you begin to suspect that there was a catch to Struldbrugg immortality?

(2) In view of the scepticism about history that Gulliver expressed in Balnibarbi, it seems strange that in Luggnagg, he should see the real advantage of immortality as the possibility of writing *objective* social and political history. As so often in *Gulliver's Travels*, extreme invective such as we find in Balnibarbi seems to result from the impossibility of achieving ideals that the historical Swift really valued. When Gulliver seeks to 'impartially draw the characters of the several successions of princes etc', he is enunciating Swift's own dream of becoming Historiographer Royal and writing an 'objective' history of the reign of Queen Anne. Yet the theoretical confusion that follows suggests his entire unsuitability for that post. **I wonder if you can discern differing theories of history enumerated on pages 254–5?**

DISCUSSION

I can find four.

(a) In Gulliver's hoping to form and direct young minds by drawing on examples of virtuous conduct, we encounter the *exemplary* theory. History provides us with examples of conduct that can be emulated or avoided.

(b) This theory is then pitted against a theory that runs through *Gulliver's Travels*, and is the structural postulate of the first two voyages, the *degeneration* theory. Over a hundred years earlier, Godfrey Goodman had argued in *The Fall of Man* (1616) that modern births were abortive attempts at earlier giant births before the 'universal decay of nature'.

(c) In the next paragraph, we are given the *cyclical* theory, the view that nations, letters, the arts, knowledge in general, rise, flourish, languish, and die, only to begin a new cycle in another part of the world. Swift's early patron, Sir William Temple, had favoured this theory in his *Essay upon the Ancient and Modern Learning*, as a way of resisting the 'modern' contention that civilization was making steady progress.

(d) Yet the *progress* theory, that the world is moving towards a state of cumulative increase in knowledge and refinement in manners is clearly implied in Gulliver's hope to see the discovery of 'the *longitude*, the *perpetual motion*, the *universal medicine*' (p. 255).

Surely the implied author is again having his sport with Gulliver, ridiculing the theoretical soup that he has cooked in expressing his high ideals for immortality? The alternative hypothesis, that this section is *not* ironic, that therefore the implied author cannot tell one historical theory from another, is unlikely.

SUMMARY

This section is cheating a little, because it will be less of a 'summary' and more of a return to the wide issues of aesthetic judgement, of unity and of 'particular' versus 'general' satire, that were raised at the opening of the chapter. I find these questions particularly urgent, and wish to tackle them now. The verdict of two hundred and fifty years of Swift criticism is that Book 3 is the least successful, because it fails to create a unified, agreeable world of the imagination. It does not transcend the material and cultural conditions that occasioned it.

These assumptions are mistaken, in my view. Without doubt, Swift pursues grave and persistent forms of misconduct and perversity in Book 3, but forms of misconduct are not homogeneous in their expression. Every era has its *characteristic* forms of political corruption, of intellectual vacuity, of economic rapacity; and for satire to be effective, it must be very specific in pinning down the stabilizing values, rules and symbols that perpetuate a particular kind of social order. Regarding the question of unity, there are a number of things to be said. In the first place, readers of this book will, I hope, share my view that Lilliput and Brobdingnag do not create unified imaginary worlds any more than the third book does. They make constant application to the extra-fictional world of contemporary social and political life, they shift in and out of different literary modes and they are ruptured by *internal contradictions*. This last point is made in the terminology of an increasingly influential French theorist called Pierre Macherey, whose *A Theory of Literary Production* argued that literature is never the seamless organic entity that some critical readings would make of it.[24] A text is an uneven, jagged production, characterized by gaps, silences, inconsistencies and blind-alleys. It never quite adds up. This is due to the way in which a text is constituted in *ideology*. Many texts commit themselves quite explicitly and patently to a set of views about the ways in which our ideas relate to the structure and maintenance of power in our society. *Gulliver's Travels* is the most *opinionated* of texts on this question and is subversive of established hierarchies. But as well as *expressing* an ideology, it is also 'placed' by an ideology of which it is a product, but which it cannot itself express, an ideology which plays round the text's boundaries and is beyond its grasp. Typically, contradictions, gaps and silences in the text suggest points at which the text is brought up sharp against its own ideological limits.

Perhaps one or two examples from the text may suggest themselves to you? Here are one or two of mine, which might clarify the point. In Lilliput, Gulliver rises in the society while also, and often consciously, exposing the corruption that makes upward social mobility undesirable and travesties social success – a contradiction that many of us live out, in varying degrees of self-awareness, all the time. Brobdingnag is presented to the reader as a society governed by a benevolent monarch whose principles are as honourable as it is possible for them to be, yet the reader's experience of how Brobdingnagian subjects actually behave is one of exploitation and sordidness. On the failure of the *spirit* of Brobdingnagian monarchical virtue to percolate downwards, the text is *silent*. In Laputa/Balnibarbi, ideological limitation is more apparent. The text has rejected speculative learning and applied science undertaken for commercial gain. To these activities, the criterion of *social utility* has been witheringly applied. Good. But to anyone who knows the subsequent history of the eighteenth-century agrarian revolution, it will be apparent that people did not 'make two ears of corn grow where one grew before' without the application of scientific principles of husbandry and technological innovation. I suspect that really innovative landlords like Coke and 'Turnip' Townshend in Norfolk, and the inventor of the seed-drill, Jethro Tull, who would probably have been assigned a cubicle in the Academy, would have had more success than Munodi in improving agricultural productivity. Robert Bakewell the Leicestershire farmer, whose experiments in scientific breeding of livestock would also have gained him a degree in Lagado, was clearly on the side of progress. Isaac Asimov has suggested that very recent scientific advance will actually produce results that are close to those Swift ridiculed as freaky and impossible: 'scientists are concerned these days with the possibility of cultivating fast-growing oily plants that can yield enough fuel to serve as a vital source of energy that . . . could be used to run generators that deliver electricity . . . we'll be getting the equivalent of sunbeams out of the equivalent of cucumbers – and the last laugh will be on Swift.'[25] Although this comment doesn't do justice to the complexity of Swift's enterprise in creating an early form of science fiction to downgrade the value of research, it is true that he was unable to see science and technology as other than on a collision course with long-established humanistic learning. Scientists were to him 'Moderns', virtuosi – 'Renaissance men gone to seed', in Lance Bertelsen's likeable phrase – speculators. This is an ideological limitation that is prescriptive over the form taken by satire in *Gulliver's Travels*.

One reason why Book 3 may seem more heterogeneous than it is, is that more significantly than looking back to early books, it anticipates themes that will be developed in Book 4. Let's get on with reading it.

4. A Voyage to the Houyhnhnms

In your reading so far, you will have come across incidents or sections of *Gulliver's Travels* where the words on the page seem to be imbued with a sinister potency to leap out and grab you, the reader, by the throat. It is not merely that the ironies are 'unstable', in Wayne Booth's word, so that they elude our capacity to read into them a single, coherent meaning. It is that the reading experience of such passages is of being led into a trap. I have dwelt on one such, the sudden switch, in 3.6, from an attack on absurd projects to an attack on the reader's cynicism about visionary politics. I mentioned then that this phenomenon has been elaborated into a theory of reading Swift – the *entrapment* theory. 'Entrapment' has been helpfully defined as 'the demonstration to the reader that his usual procedures of understanding are debilitatingly naive, simplistic, complacent, inconsistent, or inadequate in some other way'.[1] Book 4 is the ground on which Swift's traps spring most effectively.

I venture to hope that readers of *this* book are armed against a number of injudicious ways of reading *Gulliver's Travels*. I have warned against reading it as a novel and as a tight allegory; and I have tried to curtail the tendency to generalize the satire too much, arguing that there is a very particular, very detailed engagement with the practices and discourses of its own era, especially in Book 3. From the outset, I have made a point of the anti-novelistic aspects because in my experience of teaching the text, the assumptions derived from novel-reading, so difficult for modern readers to shed, lead to utter disaster in Book 4. I have also tried to orchestrate your response so that you are not searching out precise allegorical relationships between the textual particulars and some pretext, whether it be other texts, precise historical figures, or conceptual abstractions, because again, this is not a strategy that copes well with Book 4. Ideally, we need to mount a moment-by-moment guard on our responses to the text, examining critically all the assumptions we make about it, the ways in which we as readers fill in the elisions in the text. The American critic Stanley Fish has developed a theory of reading called 'affective stylistics', which involves paying word by word attention to literary sentences as we read them, so that we perceive the sentence to unfold in time as well as space.[2] This may be somewhat exaggerated and idealistic, but it does call attention to one important feature of the text of *Gulliver's Travels*: the text as a site of struggle. All too often, we think of literary texts as finished products, as the results of the conscious intention of authors who have, as it were, programmed the text's meanings into it. My experience of reading *Gulliver's Travels* 4 is of a text in which various elements struggle for mastery over the reader, creating a dynamic rather than a static object. Reading it is like looking at an optical illusion where, although there are a finite number of elements, they don't easily assume a stable configuration.

I think it would be useful to have a sense of how the text works *before* we get down to this procedure, so, departing from the established method of monitoring your initial reading, I would like you to read the entire voyage through, noting down some (albeit sketchy and provisional) answers to the following questions:

(1) **What do you take to be the meaning of the Yahoos?**
(2) **What do you take to be the meaning of the Houyhnhnms?**
(3) **How do you interpret the role of Captain Pedro de Mendez?**
(4) **What is your view of Gulliver's conduct at the end of the book, particularly the way he conducts himself towards Mendez and his own family? What do you make, for example, of pages 338–9?**

Please now read Book 4, and when you have read it, consider the three passages that I am about to set down.

The first is a very famous statement of intention Swift made in a

letter to Pope written on 29 September 1725, prior to the book's
publication. The others are statements from recent critics, and on
finishing the voyage, I want you to decide which is closer to your own
sense of the text. (Possibly neither is within a million miles of your
view. If that is the case, try to say why.)

(a) the chief end I propose to my self in all my labors is to vex the
world rather then (*sic*) divert it . . . when you think of the World
give it one lash the more at my Request. I have ever hated all
Nations professions and Communityes and all my love is towards
individualls for instance I hate the tribe of Lawyers, but I love
Councellor such a one, Judge such a one for so with Physicians (I
will not Speak of my own Trade) Soldiers, English, Scotch,
French; and the rest but principally I hate and detest that animal
called man, although I hartily love John, Peter, Thomas and so
forth. this is the system upon which I have governed my self many
years (but do not tell) and so I shall go on till I have done with
them I have got Materials Towards a Treatis proving the falsity of
that Definition *animal rationale*; and to show it should be only
rationis capax. Upon this great foundation of Misanthropy
(though not Timons manner) The whole building of my Travells
is erected.

(b) Gulliver is shown . . . to be himself part of the satire; meaning
is expressed not through any one character but through the
relationship of them all and through Gulliver's misunderstanding
of that relationship when he identifies mankind with the Yahoos
and at the same time tries to live like a Houyhnhnm, rejecting
completely the bodily instincts and passions which the Yahoos
represent. Gulliver is always too prone to take on the color of his
surroundings, and here he accepts uncritically the rational
standards of the Houyhnhnms, with the result that he . . . loses
himself in a world of extremes, seeing nothing of the larger, more
inclusive truth to be gained by moving between them.

(c) The following conclusions appear to be justified . . . Human
beings, except for minor differences, look like and behave like
Yahoos. They differ primarily in having a trace of reason, which
they use for bad ends (they pervert it), and thus are worse than the
Yahoos. Human beings like to think of themselves as rational
creatures, but if they really were rational creatures, they would
think and behave as the horses do. But they do not. By thus
attributing rationality to a non-human species Swift does not
succeed in convincing us of the superiority of horses, in this
respect, to human beings (it is evident that such a race of horses is
entirely imaginary) but simply that man is not rational. Rationality is desirable, however, even though unattainable. By making
the horses, a non-human animal, rational, Swift has produced a
double insult, or double attack, upon mankind, in its physical
being and in its mental being, and has, on the one hand, obliged
humans to identify themselves with disgusting animals, and on

the other hand, has precluded the possibility of humans' identifying themselves with horses.[3]

DISCUSSION

How far, from your reading of Book 4, do you find Swift's stated intentions realized in the text? (Perhaps you might list some salient details which would support or confute his statement.)
Swift's important statement makes three points. Swift's concern is not with *individual* human beings, but with mankind as a species; and in particular, his concern is with the claims that this species can make to rationality – is man a 'rational animal' or is the most we can say that he is *capable* of reason? Thirdly, the treatment of this and other themes will be such as to vex rather than to divert. Don't expect, therefore, to remain aloof, out of reach of the irony. Don't expect a comic book 'happy ending', such as Swift's friend John Gay has his Beggar provide in *The Beggar's Opera* because 'an Opera must end happily . . . to comply with the Taste of the Town'. (It is worth pointing out that Swift's statement of intention cannot altogether be taken at face value. For one thing, it was elaborated in response to a very different view of the satirist's calling presented by Pope in letters to Swift.)
Which of the two critical views, (b) or (c), got closest to representing your own view? (Again, it would be useful to present some evidence from your notes to support or confute them.) If you incline more towards the former, you are a 'soft' reader; if towards the latter, you are a 'hard' reader.[4] It is not too reductive, at least as a starting point, to say that most readers of Book 4 find themselves in one or other of these camps. The 'soft school' reader will stress the comic potential of the text, denying that the Houyhnhnms are any sort of an ideal for human emulation and that there is any equivalence between man and Yahoo. Captain Mendez comes closest to representing a normative humanity, living up to the full potential of mankind, whereas Gulliver's extravagant behaviour at the end is absurd and deluded. 'Hard school' readers would not accept that Swift's text searches for compromise and represents the essential goodness of human nature. Whether or not it is attainable, the hard school critic accepts that the Houyhnhnms *do* represent an ideal, judged by which human rationality is found seriously wanting. To an alarming extent, if not entirely, the man/Yahoo equation does hold; and the ending is near-tragic as Gulliver suffers under the strain of his alienation and deep sense of imperfection. There may be ways of avoiding this binarism, but it is a good starting point to accept that one or other of these tendencies dominates the reading experience of

Book 4. Consult your notes to questions 1–4 and see if you can establish from those whether you tend towards 'hard' or 'soft' reading. We will now get down to close reading, to establish how your response was formed and to see whether it will alter on further inspection of the text.

Chapter 1

Read through chapter 1, and consider Gulliver's behaviour as a man who is exploring a new country. How does the text interact with the expectations you have of it? What are your first impressions of this new territory? How do you react to Gulliver's first brush with the rational horses? Concentrate especially on the paragraph on page 272 beginning 'The two horses . . .' and pay some attention to the functioning of Gulliver's clothes.

DISCUSSION

It may be significant that in the story of Gulliver's being marooned, human nature is shown to its worst advantage. Unlike the first two voyages, where natural disaster precipitated Gulliver's fate, his predicament now is the result of morally culpable human malice. There is therefore some irony in his comfortable sense of superiority to the 'first savages [he] should meet', and in the assumption that they are to be bought off with a few baubles. Here first an anti-colonial theme is hinted at, a hatred of mercantile exploitation and its unexamined assumptions of racial superiority, which will be deafeningly loud by the end of the voyage. Gulliver's first impressions of the Yahoos are overwhemingly negative: 'I never beheld in all my travels so disagreeable an animal, nor one against which I naturally conceived so strong an antipathy' (p. 270). There is absolutely no similarity perceived between the Yahoos and human beings initially. Yahoo hairiness, pendulous breasts and agility mark them off as non-human, and at this point the modern reader is quite secure in regarding them as a species of monkey. Noticeably, it is Gulliver, not the Yahoo, who commits the first act of open aggression, refusing to give the benefit of a doubt between 'curiosity or mischief'. I find it difficult, however, to share the tender sensibilities of certain critics who actively sympathize with the Yahoos: creatures who scurry up trees and 'discharge their excrements' upon one's head will never get my vote as pets of the year! And then Gulliver meets his first Houyhnhnm.

Why, in your view, should horses be fixed on as the animal species to be endowed with reason?

DISCUSSION

Perhaps the key sentence is this one: 'I was amazed to see such actions and behaviour in brute beasts, and concluded with myself, that if the inhabitants of this country were endued with a proportionable degree of reason, they must needs be the wisest people upon earth' (p. 271). That sentence testifies clearly to an established eighteenth-century hierarchy. Men are superior in the creation to 'brute beasts'. They occupy a higher rung on the ladder of being because, of course, they are rational. Within that hierarchy, horses have a precise semiotic significance; that is, they function as signs of culturally coded and conventionally agreed values. Horses are faithful beasts of burden, gaining a certain nobility through their unquestioning loyalty, unstinting industry and enormous social utility. They are not, however, intelligent. Nowadays, we are familiar with the concept of animal intelligence, and the higher primates are known to be very intelligent indeed. *Gulliver's Travels* shows that primates were not then thought to challenge horses in the anthropocentrically devised league table of being, but neither were horses serious contenders for promotion to the first division of rationality. Horses with varying expressions, with social forms, with articulate language, were an affront to all the certainties of eighteenth-century ontology, the more challenging because, unlike monkeys, their signification was precisely understood. Unlike Gulliver, this horse does not need to resort to violence to subdue other life-forms to his will: he possesses an innate authority. When in a very short space of time, Gulliver is actually 'expect[ing] his farther commands', we can imagine how eighteenth-century readers must have broken out into a sweat of indignation.

The passage on page 272 that I asked you to look at is a particularly interesting one. Gulliver is not at this point aware of why the horses take such a lively interest in his clothes, nor is the first-time reader; but anticipating a little, I will say that clothes are one heavily contested area in the fourth voyage. Gulliver's clothes are a prime example of the struggle for mastery in the text that I discussed in the preamble. What is intriguing the Houyhnhnms is Gulliver's resemblance to a Yahoo, except that his clothes conceal the extent of it. The uncovered areas of his body differ only in very minor respects of colour, hirsuteness and texture. These differences would allow the Houyhnhnms to classify him as of the same species, perhaps a different genus. But the clothes, which in their naiveté they take to be natural, complicate that judgement. Already then, there is a confrontation of a 'real' but artificial life-style, that of Gulliver the European, and a 'fictional' but natural life-style, that of the

The rational horses.
An illustration from Book 4 of the Hague
edition (1727) of *Gulliver's Travels*.

Houyhnhnms. We have already learned that the land is not under artificial cultivation, but rather is 'divided by long rows of trees, not regularly planted, but naturally growing'. And of course, one advantage with horses is that what you see is what you get. There are no hidden flaws, such as could be concealed by clothes. We'll come back to this point later.

The chapter ends with one of those very funny 'take me to your leader' conversations with which science fiction has made us familiar. Filthy and beshitten, Gulliver makes a speech to the creatures that he has decided must be magicians (as the more believable alternative to their being rational horses!), who, for their parts, are astonished to hear him speak at all (since a quasi-Yahoo breaking into articulate speech is as unbelievable to them as a speaking monkey is to Gulliver), but are compelled by their pacifist manners to 'listen with great attention'. To the reader, it is fairly obvious that the Houyhnhnms are not going to be much impressed by a present of a knife and a bracelet, nor are they ever likely to permit Gulliver to ride them 'as if he were a real horse'. For an instant, Houyhnhnm and human are on equivalent terms, both astonished at the rational capacities of the other. Already, though, ominous signs of hierarchy are appearing, as Houyhnhnm language is praised for its expressive capacity, as Gulliver is taught to neigh rather than teaching the natives to speak the King's English, and as his weariness proves him physically inferior to the stalwart Houyhnhnm. What a reversal of the colonial theme of the white man travelling to foreign lands to civilize and convert the natives! How ironic that Gulliver should begin his study of Houyhnhnm language by practising the very word, above all others, that he should resist, the word 'Yahoo'. This is the word that the discourse seeks to foist onto him, as a definition: Man equals Yahoo.

Chapters 2–4

As a response to this section, I would like you to consider the following questions:

(1) **Why do you think Gulliver struggles to avoid the appellation 'Yahoo'?**

(2) **Develop, if you can, the issue of Gulliver's clothes that we introduced in the previous section.**

(3) **Look especially at the opening paragraph of chapter 4 (p. 286). How adequate do you find the Houyhnhnm conception of language? Is the passage a satire on impoverished linguistics, or is Gulliver's language the target of the satire?**

DISCUSSION

(1) No reader can be unaware of Gulliver's struggle against the appellation 'Yahoo' that the Houyhnhnms are so eager to foist onto him. It is as if the discourse is determined to make that label stick, while Gulliver himself tries to avoid it. I'm not sure if it's even correct to say that the *implied author* wants to identify Gulliver with the Yahoos. The struggle seems to be so evanescent that it is perhaps best located in the 'unconscious' of the text, where 'unconscious' designates an area of meaning that isn't controlled by the author or by the implied author.[5]

There is, I think, a very important point at issue here. Allow me to digress briefly, to expound the view of a seminal French historian whose work has been influential on recent literary critics, Michel Foucault. In his *Les Mots et les choses* (1966), translated as *The Order of Things*, Foucault argued that in the late seventeenth century, and into the eighteenth, modes of apprehending the world were gradually changing. The earlier way of knowing (Foucault's term is *episteme*) is characterized by a system of resemblances between all the items of creation; whereas in the Classical episteme that succeeded it, the world came to be analysed in terms of identity and difference. Only by means of measurement and order can it now be established that one item resembles another; and the objective of knowledge will be to discriminate rather than to draw together in a net of similarity. Three forms of analysis come to dominate the Classical episteme: the science of calculation (*mathesis*), the science of origins (*genesis*) and the science of classification (*taxonomia*). In the eighteenth century, the first influential attempts were made to classify living species in systematic ways by Linnaeus and others. In the following difficult but illuminating passage, Foucault comments on the way in which the naming of species becomes more 'scientific' in this period through the filtering out of forms of knowledge no longer considered relevant to classification:

> The Classical age gives history a quite different meaning: that of undertaking a meticulous examination of things themselves for the first time, and then of transcribing what it has gathered in smooth, neutralized, and faithful words. It is understandable that the first form of history constituted in this period of 'purification' should have been the history of nature. For its construction requires only words applied, without intermediary, to things themselves. The documents of this new history are not other words, texts or records, but unencumbered spaces in which things are juxtaposed: herbariums, collections, gardens; the locus of this history is a non-temporal rectangle in which, stripped of all commentary, of all enveloping language, creatures present themselves one beside another, their surfaces visible, grouped

according to their common features, and thus already virtually analysed, and bearers of nothing but their own individual names. It is
often said that the establishment of botanical gardens and zoological
collections expressed a new curiosity about exotic plants and animals.
In fact, these had already claimed men's interest for a long while.
What had changed was the space in which it was possible to see them
and from which it was possible to describe them. To the Renaissance,
the strangeness of animals was a spectacle: it was featured in fairs, in
tournaments, in fictitious or real combats, in reconstitutions of
legends in which the bestiary displayed its ageless fables. The natural
history room and the garden, as created in the Classical period,
replace the circular procession of the 'show' with the arrangement of
things in a 'table'. What came surreptitiously into being between the
age of the theatre and that of the catalogue was not the desire for
knowledge, but a new way of connecting things both to the eye and to
discourse. A new way of making history.[6]

Notice the emphasis placed, in the above quotation, on the relationship between *words* and *objects* in the natural world, which we
have already discerned as of central importance to Swift's writing. It
is precisely the question of taxonomy, of classification, that is at issue
in these chapters. On the basis of resemblance, the mare decides that
Gulliver is a Yahoo, bringing him face to face with that un-
prepossessing species to facilitate the comparison. At that point,
Gulliver is himself first struck by the resemblance, except that this is
immediately distanced by Gulliver's sense that it holds best for
'savage nations'. On the criterion of diet, it becomes apparent that
Gulliver is neither Houyhnhnm nor Yahoo, since he can prosper on
the fare of neither. And on page 277, a strong point is made of his
instinctive repulsion from the Yahoos: 'I never saw any sensitive
being so detestable on all accounts.' Gulliver's intermediate status is
recorded in the fact that he is quartered in a stable somewhere
between Houyhnhnm and Yahoo territory. On page 280, it is made
clear that to Houyhnhnm perception, Gulliver is superior to the
Yahoo, through his 'teachableness, civility and cleanliness', and
other 'marks of a rational creature'. Yet the Houyhnhnm is reluctant
to allow these differences to be the basis of a reclassification.
Linnaeus's system for classification was based on selecting structures
of plants (say, the reproductive system) which would be taken as
relevant to a consideration of similarities and differences. Here,
though the Houyhnhnm can detect differences, he refuses them
relevance. Thus, he cannot understand how a 'parcel of brutes' could
sail a ship, since the Yahoos couldn't do it. He concludes that
Gulliver's words do not express any true proposition, rather than
concluding that he is not a Yahoo. Again, on page 282, Gulliver is
allowed to have 'some glimmerings of Reason', but this is not

considered to be a constituent difference between human and Yahoo. Rather, it leads the Houyhnhnm towards a proto-evolutionary theory. Gulliver is a 'perfect Yahoo'. The chapter ends with Gulliver pleading to be treated as a species different from the Yahoos, aware that his well-being will depend on it. The final paragraph of chapter 3 (p. 285) clearly enacts the terminological struggle, as Gulliver first refers to himself as a 'creature', then a 'rational animal', then refuses the term 'Yahoo' by admitting a physical resemblance but claiming a difference in essential nature, and finally collapsing into accepting a man/Yahoo/brute equation.

(2) There is, then, a struggle between Gulliver and the Houyhnhnm for mastery over the latter's identity; and something more difficult to specify: a refusal, on the part of the discourse (i.e. the writing that embodies the story) actually to *retain* what has been decided about this from one moment to the next. No wonder, then, that the text is so fluid. A vital, but uncertain signifier in all this, is Gulliver's apparel.

At the outset, clothes conceal the true extent of Gulliver's resemblance to the Yahoos (p. 276). They therefore help to guarantee his human rights, which depend on maintaining his separateness from them. On the other hand, clothes can be interpreted as a sign of human willingness to deceive, symbolic of man's desire to cover his unregenerate nature. Pulling on and off his gloves seems to the Houyhnhnms a mysterious and magical transformation. Reliance on what is clearly a contingent and inessential mark of identity, not part of the definition of 'essential' humanity, produces anxiety in Gulliver. When his 'deception' is discovered, the Houyhnhnms see this as a rupture of identity, a proliferation of difference: 'I was not the same thing when I slept as I appeared to be at other times; that his valet assured him, some part of me was white, some yellow, at least not so white, and some brown.' Gulliver's explanation for the wearing of clothes is exploited by the Houyhnhnm to show that his concept of nature is equally ruptured and unclear, based on a misunderstood scission between nature and culture. 'Nature' does not teach us to conceal our genitals; culture does, the Biblical story of Adam and Eve accounting for our learned shame at nudity. Houyhnhnms are, according to their own etymology, the 'Perfection of Nature', entirely present and self-identical to nature. Incapable of 'saying the thing that is not', their language does not introduce dangerous plurality of meaning – polysemy, in modern critical parlance. Quite obviously, it is far too simple to say that the text equates man and Yahoo, or that Swift thinks men are Yahoos, or anything of the kind. What seems truer is that the Houyhnhnms have a mode of being that is not divided from nature by culturally-created artifice.

(3) This passage is a good example of the kind of Swiftian irony that, to return to the terms used in the opening of this chapter, most unsettles the reader and is most effective in challenging the adequacy of her/his reading procedures. The reader is beginning to be aware that Houyhnhnm simplicity is a powerful weapon against human pseudo-complexity, self-deception, hypocrisy and irrationality. Houyhnhnm linguistics are appealing in their straightforwardness: 'the use of speech was to make us understand one another, and to receive information of facts' seems devastatingly comprehensive, solving at a stroke all the tortuousness of eighteenth-century philosophical attempts to fix a relationship between language and the world. So, in the first place, it seems that the Houyhnhnms have again exposed a weakness in our culture – the divisions that exist between words and their meanings, the doubleness, duplicity in our ways of using words. But think again. When you 'say the thing that is not', are you always *lying*? What about when you are writing fiction? Or using words that have no real referent – 'unicorn', 'the present King of France'? If you use a counterfactual language, such as the language of morality – 'promises ought to be kept' – are you then within the Houyhnhnm definition of the use of words? A linguistic definition that would not permit the writing of *Gulliver's Travels* is surely one that the implied author of this passage could not endorse, and nor altogether can the reader. In the last sentence of the paragraph, however, the irony moves in a different direction. Condescendingly, Gulliver comments on the Houyhnhnms' rusticity and lack of polish in not being more adept as liars. Here, we sense that the implied author is in league with us against Gulliver, smiling at his unworthy superiority, and this is quite manageable. Less manageable is the sense that if we as readers accept the linguistic theory on which the criticism of Gulliver is partially based, we are also giving up the reading competences that allow us to understand that criticism.

Space prevents further discussion of chapter 4, but I suggest that you might refer back to what we said about 'theriophily' in discussing 2.5, and consider how theriophilic arguments are being used here to mortify human dignity and belittle human pride. Show how this style of argument is mapped onto the struggle between the terms man: Yahoo: horse: Houyhnhnm and the apportioning of reason between these categories.

Chapters 5–7

You will notice the general formal resemblance between this section and Book 2.6, when under questioning from the King of Brobding-nag, Gulliver is finally forced to reveal the 'truth' about English institutions. Here, it seems, there is no reluctance to reveal this 'truth', and to produce a fundamental, devastating indictment of our social structure. Two questions present themselves at this point:

(1) The question of genre. What is your view of the savagery and absolutism of this attack? Can it be contained by the term 'satire' or is it too uncontrolled for that?
(2) The question of narrative transmission. Has Gulliver as narrator been too far absorbed by the voice of the implied author or is it that Gulliver's narration has been *affected* by his stay in Houyhnhnm-land?

DISCUSSION

(1) At first sight, it may seem that this is mere vituperation, invective that has lost the restraints conferred by the artistic conventions of satire. One is incensed by Gulliver's portrayal of our legal institutions and perhaps even of military aggression in such a biased way. To banish the possibility of ever obtaining justice as finally as the text does is to travesty the belief that we may have of living in at least a reasonably fair and equitable society, which is at the root of our concept of 'civilization'. I think there is, in the end, some truth in such a view – the famous 'savage indignation' that, as Swift's tombstone asserts, lacerated his breast. Yet indignation is carefully structured in the writing, precisely to provoke in the reader a crescendo of mounting anger and discomfort.

(2) The discourse of this section (pp. 291–306) represents a set of 'minutes' or shorthand notes of conversations conducted over two years, so that there is initially a plausible reason for the coagulated texture. Reference to 'our barbarous English' (p. 292) gives an early warning of how Gulliver is positioned as a convert to Houyhnhnm values (further explored on pp. 305–6). The past tense being used here to tell the story is not quite the past progressive (the common narrative past tense), but rather a more absolute past which is quite affected by the narrator's present position as Houyhnhnm convert. In other words, he is biased, because he is telling the story not 'as it happened' but through the value-system he has now wholly absorbed. I think there *is* a gradual change in the narrator's nature as Book 4 progresses, as assimilation to Houyhnhnm ways of thinking

advances. This is an additional source of complexity and movement in the final voyage. As would-be Houyhnhnm, he can no longer enter imaginatively into nodes of religious controversy such as the consecrated elements of bread and wine in the Eucharist, or the use of music in church services, or the veneration of the Crucifix, or the precise nature of ecclesiastical vestments. On page 292, he can only represent these literally, as they would appear to someone so far outside the culture that all symbolic significance is lost. As an apprentice Houyhnhnm, Gulliver gains some of the freedom he possessed as a giant in Lilliput, so that he can represent the causes of war not exactly 'truthfully', but as they might appear if stripped of all the justificatory rhetoric of the council chamber. In this account, wars originate in Caesarism and naked ambition. The Houyhnhnm's theriophilic intervention – 'for your mouths lying flat with your faces, you can hardly bite each other to any purpose' – gives Gulliver the excuse to produce another of the catalogues with which the text abounds. Pause in your reading now to analyse this catalogue. Is there any structure in it, or is it sheer aggregation? How does it affect you?

It will remind us of Gulliver's earlier portrait in 2.7 of the devastation produced by gunpowder, but it is even more of an expressionistic collage, giving the progress of a naval and military encounter in thirty seconds. Clearly, there are some terms that you need to be expert to know – 'carabines', 'culverins', 'undermines', 'countermines' – and these impart authenticity to the description. There is also a clear time-scheme moving from armaments to the battle and its terrors to the aftermath. Random detail and energy is therefore carefully planned and structured. To Swift, there was a close connection between professionalism, with its accompanying trade-talk, and brutality or crude exploitation of power.[7] I am left with an impression of tremendous energy misused, and am sickened by the idea that raining corpses is a source of 'diversion' to some people. (But observe the behaviour of the crowd that gathers round to get a better view of any motorway accident! In Los Angeles, very long traffic jams are caused by what is chillingly referred to as 'spectator slowing'.) The Houyhnhnm is also disgusted at this, and it leads him to an interesting philosophical speculation. Again, humans are in some sense *more* malicious than Yahoos, because Yahoos, like *gnnayhs* and stones act according to the dictates of their natures. It seems that men are endowed, not with reason (which must always co-operate with nature in securing what nature desires for the good of the species), but with a faculty that parodies Reason by monstrously magnifying the vices that our fallen natures prompt us to indulge. So, as we approach the mid-point of the Book, mankind is represented as being permanently exiled from nature by the malign influence of his culture.

There follows a vitriolic attack on the legal profession. Why do you think that the law is so singled out for satirical attention? Is there anything contradictory in this attack?

DISCUSSION

The professions are age-old targets of satire, perennial objects of indignation and ridicule on account of their jargon-mongering and money-grubbing tendencies. By deliberately coining obscure, supposedly 'expert' registers of language (so the attacks go) the professions create a no-go linguistic area where laymen will not venture by themselves, but rather will pay to employ guides. This section of *Gulliver's Travels* is clearly written out of a venerable satiric tradition, but as usual in Swift, the screw is given an extra turn by the extreme opposition posited between 'truth' and legal practice. 'Truth', the clear and distinct, immediately apprehensible facts of a case, is seen to be the main danger to the legal profession, which will go to any lengths to conceal it. Through tortuous legal argument and the multiplying of procedure, the legal system must become a self-generating discourse, immune at all stages to the penetration of 'truth', even if at times this costs money: 'I have known several [Judges] refuse a large bribe from the side where justice lay, rather than injure the *Faculty* by doing anything unbecoming their nature or their office' (p. 296).

At this point, I wish to raise a question that has been in the back of my mind for some time. Do you see the satiric standpoint outlined above as conservative, or as radical, in political terms? This is, I think, a difficult question to answer. We must beware of projecting our own political alignments directly onto the text, because distinctions that we might make and understand (say, between left-wing and right-wing political positions) do not map onto the eighteenth century in any straightforward way. At the risk of paradox, I would say that Swift's stance is that of the radical conservative. The Houyhnhnms have no need of a legal system, because 'Nature and Reason were sufficient guides for a reasonable animal'. With this alignment, no serious structural division of opinion can ever occur in a community. Significantly, the dispute that Swift chooses to illustrate legal malpractice is one over property rights: 'if my neighbour hath a mind to my cow . . .'. But how does that cow come to be mine in the first place? Vituperation here does not extend as far as to attack the notion of private property. While cows continue to be yours and mine, it is difficult to imagine that property disputes will not occur. Arguably, property creates the law and its abuses. There are, then, strict limits to the seeming radicalism of the satire here.

Chapter 6 forces the reader to engage certain strands of early eighteenth-century ideology presented in unadorned and straightforward forms, even if pressurized by satiric indignation. I suggest that you try to hone your wits against them. **What is your opinion of the views of money, luxury, illness and medical care that Gulliver presents to the Houyhnhnm here?**

DISCUSSION

To treat these points thoroughly, it would be necessary to consider theories of money, price, value, utility and exchange as these had developed up to Swift's day, which space does not permit. I want to comment only very briefly here.[8] The discourse is propelled by moral indignation into areas where it is not perhaps entirely thought out. As Robinson Crusoe had discovered on his island, money in itself is merely a substitute in the mechanism of exchange. It is of no value where it cannot be exchanged, in territories where the prince's head stamped on coinage means absolutely nothing. Voyage literature provides opportunities for moral condemnation of miserliness, avarice, the stockpiling of money, condemnation which derives its authority from Biblical texts about the service of God and Mammon (Matthew 6:24). Houyhnhnmland, like Crusoe's island, provides the ideally remote location to reinforce a text like 'Consider the lilies of the field, how they grow; they toil not, neither do they spin', which is behind Gulliver's attack on luxury here. Actually, although there was not yet a systematic science of political economy in Swift's day, understanding of economic matters had progressed well beyond the point where it was feasible to lament the division of labour, or to deny the importance of money as a determinant of wealth. Equally unconvincing is the analysis of illness entirely in moral terms. We do certainly abuse our bodies, but not all illnesses are attributable to that. On firmer ground is the attack on contemporary medical practice, which you might have registered as a return to the objects of satire in the previous voyage. Believe it or not, around 1719, Dr John Woodward, whose name I have mentioned before, had concluded that a build-up of 'biliose salts' in the stomach was responsible for most physical illness and had prescribed murderous courses of 'vomits' to evacuate them. He became embroiled with another physician, Dr John Freind, who thought that in certain circumstances, purges were necessary to the cure of smallpox. The question of whether the body should be purged orally or anally provoked a personal combat between Woodward and Dr Mead, a supporter of Freind. The use of italicized technical terms here is a good indication that the satire has become very particular and local. And indeed, truth is stranger here than anything Swift's satire could invent. You may feel as I do that the incidence of catalogues as a stylistic feature in this chapter suggests a form of rhetorical brow-beating which comes to the rescue of extreme and unconvincing positions. On page 299, for instance, we are said to support luxury by exporting necessities and importing 'the materials of diseases, folly and vice', causing 'vast numbers of our people to seek their livelihood' by practices that include 'forswearing', 'star-gazing' and 'free-thinking'. This is a curious farrago of mercantilist argument, moral satire and exaggeration. Mercantilism was a complex of late seventeenth-century theory and practice that encouraged a positive balance of trade by routing trade through certain governmentally sponsored restrictions. These encouraged merchants to import raw materials rather than manufactured goods and to export manufactured goods rather than commodities. Above all else, mercantilists advocated embargos on luxury goods because in paying for these in specie, the importing nation was depleting its money supply, paying the wages of foreign workers and taking work away from domestic workers. Mercantilism is intimately bound up with colonialism, because colonies provide the supply of raw materials as well as the markets for the subsequently manufactured goods. To Swift, this kind of trading relationship was destroying a potentially prosperous Irish woollen industry by forcing the Irish to export wool, a rich natural resource, and to import the woollen goods that they could have been making themselves. In other words, England's colonial attitude to Ireland, which denied equal trading rights to Irish merchants, forced the Irish onto the unfavourable side of the mercantile transaction.

There is something excessive about the satire in this chapter. If Ministers of State behaved with the kind of consistency imputed to them on page 302, they wouldn't be especially dangerous.[9] As we learn at the end of the chapter, Houyhnhnm society is a rigid caste society, but unlike ours, social elevation is commensurate with inherited ability. This is a genuine aristocracy. Gulliver's description of English nobility is again such a caricature that the reader may be beginning to suspect that he is unhinged. Infuriatingly, the text anticipates us. Disarmingly, Gulliver explains that he speaks with the zeal of a convert. The Houyhnhnms so impressed him with their virtue and love of truth that he wished to remain amongst them. This tactic allows him to claim that, if anything, he has understated the case against humans that we have been dismissing as grossly overstated. We begin to understand what Swift meant when he said that he wrote the book to 'vex the world'!

Chapters 8–10

I should like you now to follow the account of the Yahoos given in chapters 7 and 8 (pp. 306–15), arriving, if you can, at some conclusion as to what relationship is being said to obtain between Yahoos and humans. In particular, consider the serio-comic incident on pages 314–15, where Gulliver is sexually assaulted by an impassioned female Yahoo. When you have completed that to your own satisfaction, please read pages 315–28, noting down as much as you can about Houyhnhnm culture and society. Thumb through the earlier chapters to gather information; and at this stage, try to stick to description rather than evaluation of the Houyhnhnm community. Remember that what is omitted from the analysis of Houyhnhnm society might be as significant as what is included, so think about the various industries, institutions, forms of employment and culture that make *our* society what it is. This will furnish a basis for comparison.

DISCUSSION

Gathering up clues from the earlier chapters, I find a society that has a simple architecture, functional interior furnishing and design, is cattle-rearing and is vegetarian (though food is processed). Judging by their fastidious eating habits and the 'modest' behaviour of the young, the Houyhnhnms value etiquette and decorum. In general, with their hoof-striking rituals and dinner parties, they seem thoroughly socialized. Houyhnhnm society is clearly hierarchical. Status and rank are carefully preserved, as is shown in 4.2 when the old steed 'who seemed to be of quality' is received by 'our horse' with 'great civility'. His sledge is the Houyhnhnm equivalent of the opulent equipage of the eighteenth-century gentry. Indeed, the entire ceremony of his reception is closely modelled on that of the eighteenth-century squire receiving a nobleman into his house. There are masters and servants in Houyhnhnm society – and depending on what we decide about the status of Yahoos, we might consider them to be a slave caste. Although they have an expressive language, the Houyhnhnms are illiterate and have no written culture. Later chapters establish Houyhnhnm society as simple and communal, rooted in nature. There is an uncomplicated husbandry, producing oats, hay and milk. Technologically primitive (they 'know not the use of iron'), they can fashion instruments with flint, but have no sophisticated agricultural tools like ploughs. Beyond this, we tend to be recording what there isn't in Houyhnhnmland rather than what there is. There is no manufacturing industry and consequently no internal or external trade. There is no currency and therefore no financial system, taxation system or the like. Again, as in 4.6, this engages the mercantilist bias in the economic thinking of Swift's era. Mercantilists believed international trade to be part of God's intention as expressed in a providential pattern designed to promote international peace and friendship.[10] If no Houyhnhnms are merchants or traders, this must be a significant omission. Even more significant, there is no conception of a life beyond the grave, and therefore no organized religion.

An adjective that may have occurred to you when describing this society is 'Spartan'. If so, I think that this is very accurate.[11] Accounts of the constitution and social organization of Sparta were conveyed by Plutarch's *Life of Lycurgus* and Xenophon's *Constitution of the Lacedaemonians*, both works that Swift knew well. The Spartan ideal of conduct is present not only in Book 4 but also in Brobdingnag and in the original constitution of Lilliput, before the onset of corruption. The Spartans favoured a rigid caste system, because it ensured unity in the ruling class and stability in the state. They assumed that the state takes its complexion from the moral natures of its individual members, so that much emphasis must be placed on the moral training of rulers. Stability is ensured by suppressing all potential destabilizing factors. Wants are curtailed by severe self-discipline and the discouragement of all forms of consumerism. Individual affection and romantic sentiment are not permitted to get in the way of collective ideals. No parental ties of affection are permitted; rather, a less personal friendship and benevolence create a public-spirited and conformist society. Education becomes in Sparta and in Houyhnhnmland a form of ethical and physical conditioning, based on privation and hardiness, a constant round of work and occupation. Clearly, an extensive written culture would be a very powerful destabilizing factor, because it would encourage the individualism of private study. Art that was critical rather than didactic or panegyric (i.e. devoted to praise) would also be threatening to the social fabric of such an authoritarian society. It is no surprise, therefore, that the Spartan Houyhnhnms express contempt for the accumulation of books. Like Spartan society, the Houyhnhnms are regulated ('governed' would not be the correct term, because it would suggest the inadequacy of self-control) by only a single institution, a 'Representative Council'. (Notice that we are not told

how its membership is arrived at.) A final macabre comparison can
be found in the fact that the Spartans had a 'final solution' for dealing
with their own helots (slave class): they were to be systematically
slaughtered by a secret service appointed for the purpose. The
Houyhnhnms too are debating ways of dealing with the Yahoo
question.

The question we now have to confront, perhaps the most complex
question that *Gulliver's Travels* raises, is what are we to make of the
Houyhnhnms and their form of civilization? What I would suggest is
that we frame a number of propositions (say, four) that express
possible views of the Houyhnhnms — not necessarily views that we
take, but views that will initiate thought or discussion. You should
consider the pros and cons of each, and try to arrive at a decision as to
which best meets the case. I will discuss two of them below.
(1) Houyhnhnm society is not presented as a society to be emulated
any more than Yahoo 'society' is. What is being recommended is a
middle way.
(2) Houyhnhnm society represents a rational utopia.
(3) Houyhnhnm society is set up only as a means of satirizing human
society.
(4) Houyhnhnm society is an ideal society.

DISCUSSION

Proposition 2: there is no doubt that this is a society governed by
rational principles. As page 315 makes clear, the Houyhnhnms are
wholly governed by Reason, and by a form of it that is 'clear and
distinct' in Descartes' phrase; that is to say, Reason is not here a
synonym for argument. Whether or not it is a utopia depends, not
surprisingly, on what the reader takes a 'utopia' to be. Certainly,
imaginary societies in previous literature have had their effect on the
shaping of Houyhnhnmland. Sparta has already been discussed, and
we could add to accounts of Sparta Plato's *Republic* and Sir Thomas
More's *Utopia*, both influential on Swift. Two questions present
themselves, however. How attainable does a society have to be to call
itself a 'utopia' and how desirable? The fundamental issue is that
raised in all of our propositions above: is the purpose of utopia
mainly satirical, or mainly political? It has been argued that an
utopia is a fictional society or state that confronts one of the central
problems of politics: how to relate a society's wants to the satisfactions that it can provide.[12] My wants may fail to be satisfied either by
a material scarcity of satisfactions or by some sociological uneven-
ness in the way what society affords is divided up, or by both. To

some commentators, the true utopist confronts this problem head-on, and to the extent that he avoids it, he is not a genuine utopist. On this view, utopias are programmatic. They are not escapist or fantastic, but rather they build in ways of controlling the consequences of deficiencies in provision and of human imperfection. Writers who engage with their fictional societies in this way presumably see them as at least conceivably attainable. At the least, they are suggesting a direction for social reform to take. Other writers do not accept that utopian thinking is properly as political as this: utopia is 'nowhere but in the mind . . . its only function is to measure the present by an unchallengeable ideal'.[13] Since *Gulliver's Travels* presents a society of rational horses, it is closer to utopia in the second sense than in the first. In the political sense, *Gulliver's Travels* is not a very convincing utopia. In Houyhnhnmland, the question of wants versus satisfactions is raised, admittedly, but not with much rigour. On page 318, we are simply told that the Representative Council, on a four-yearly basis, meets to do any redistribution necessary. Because the Houyhnhnms do not want much, the question of scarcity doesn't really arise. What is surprising is that children are regarded exactly in the same way as other material scarcities. And this leads on to the question of desirability. We are accustomed to think, perhaps rather loosely, of utopias as ultimately desirable societies, even 'perfect' societies. Yet that is not usually my experience of reading them. They project a total social environment, highly organized and hedged in with rules and sanctions designed to promote collective happiness. (More's *Utopia* is a good example, if you wish to follow this up.) Any manifestations of individualism – conscience, desire for privacy or freedom, the desire to exercise choice, the desire to criticize, the desire to experience change – is a considerable problem for utopists. In *Gulliver's Travels*, since the Houyhnhnms do not appear to be subject to human emotions, the inner life (which might be the source of individualism) is edited out. Again, since it doesn't squarely confront the fundamental issues faced by utopists, I wonder if it can be correct to call Houyhnhnmland a utopia?

Proposition 4: this is ambiguous. Does 'ideal' mean simply 'the product of an idea'? The society is imagined into being in order to ridicule man's pride in his own rational nature. Or is it stronger than that? Does it mean that the society is in any way desirable? And if so, in what way? For Gulliver, who is our guide and sometimes our representative in Houyhnhnmland, there is no doubt that it is an ideal society in this stronger sense. Houyhnhnms are perfect creatures who are to be loved, venerated and as far as possible imitated.

The extent of his assimilation is underlined on page 327, when he speaks of the reverse narcissism that has led him to hate the sight of his own face and to imitate the 'gait and gesture' of the Houyhnhnms. It is deeply regrettable that humans are not Houyhnhnms and all we can do is take every step to narrow the gap.

Some readers react very intensely to Gulliver's behaviour in this voyage, seeing his actions as a betrayal of human nature and detesting the life-form to which he subsumes himself. As we saw at the beginning of the chapter, 'soft' readers of the book go the length of arguing that there is an ironic subversion of the Houyhnhnms and of Gulliver's adoring attitude to them. The 'implied author' is again involved in a conspiracy with the reader against his protagonist and his perfectly rational creatures. What support can be found for this view? If you haven't already done so, give this some thought before reading what I have to say.

We might argue that there is great value in the emotional, non-rational side of human nature. The Houyhnhnms inhabit a cold, anaemic society that it is quite impossible for a human to envy or admire. Passion is what creates love, beauty, true art; and in so far as the Houyhnhnms do not have these, they are not . . . human! That seems circular. A more powerful argument often advanced is that the way the Houyhnhnms treat Gulliver and/or the Yahoos could not conceivably be intended to be admirable. All readers must deplore this and loathe the Houyhnhnms as a result. (Some readers have even argued that the Yahoos are a subjugated class – high-potential low-achievers who are enslaved by the Houyhnhnms in a way typical of British colonialism or Irish policy.[14]) In chapter 9, the Council debate about exterminating the Yahoos, which makes the clement resolution merely to castrate them, is not so different from the Lilliputian resolution merely to blind Gulliver. Is there not a sense in which the Houyhnhnms society is condemned for failing to treat Gulliver with proper respect? The Council comes close to blaming humans for the existence of the Yahoos by invoking a tradition that the Yahoos are degenerate foreigners (connecting with a theme of degeneration that has threaded through the entire work – see, for example, the 'little old treatise' that Gulliver finds in Brobdingnag, pp. 177–8). This might be regarded as special pleading, since in all other respects, the Houyhnhnms are a very *un*historical race. Is there not something ironic in Gulliver's thinking, on pages 324–5, that he does not 'feel the treachery or inconstancy of a friend, nor the injuries of a secret or open enemy', since at the Council, he is, in human terms, being betrayed? Indeed, can't his Houyhnhnm master be accused of malfeasance at an early stage in the voyage, since on page 284, he consents to keep the secret of Gulliver's clothes (why should he?), but a paragraph later is treating him with civility merely to exploit him more efficiently? Does the decision to expel Gulliver for fear he may become a Yahoo Spartacus (p. 328) not establish the lack of self-confidence in their society? Is that a rational decision?

I find that in the end, I want to reject that reading, which (going back to the distinction with which we began the chapter, between 'soft' and 'hard' readings) is clearly a 'soft' reading. Ralph W. Rader has commented that this view is 'as if one were to set a building afire in order to put it out'.[15] Why imagine a species of rational horses who can serve as a devastating critique of the belief that humans are rational, only to undermine them? Why expend energy showing the inadequacies of creatures who don't exist? **We might look at the passage on page 331, Gulliver's leave-taking. Try to work out what the 'soft' and 'hard' readings of this passage might be.**

DISCUSSION

Soft
In this house of soft readers, there's not a dry eye to be found! As humans, we must applaud the ties of affection that Gulliver has developed and find value in the physiology of emotion – 'mine eyes flowing with tears, and my heart quite sunk with grief'. Our hearts are full of pity for the small recompense he gets from the Houyhnhnms for such unstinting loyalty. Creatures who are capable of sending him out alone on a wide, wide sea are surely deserving of contempt rather than admiration.

Hard
Sentimental tosh! If only the soft reader would realize that it is entirely rational to act in one's own interest. It is not in the Houyhnhnm interest to retain Gulliver because he will contaminate perfect rationality. Already, indeed, he has had an influence; his master actually found himself, at the Council, proposing a suggestion (castration) that came from Gulliver. As for this passage, it testifies to Gulliver's weakness more than anything else. Just like a frail human to allow his emotional nature to get the better of him, to idolize a species that he can never succeed in imitating. It isn't rational to be grateful for such small mercies as the Houyhnhnms are prepared to show him.

I find the latter more convincing than the former, but perhaps both neglect the dynamics of the passage. If we read as above, our indignation is aroused, either at Houyhnhnm cruelty (soft) or at Gulliver's emotional weakness (hard), but that indignation is evidence of involvement in the story, at least partial surrender to the fiction. If, instead, we regard Gulliver and the Houyhnhnms as counters in a satirical game, our reaction will be more dangerous to the implied author. Gulliver anticipates that readers will react against him here. 'I am not ignorant how much I have been censured for mentioning this last particular.' But he disarms us by putting it in terms of degree of belief: 'For my detractors are pleased to think it improbable, that so illustrious a person should descend to give so great a mark of distinction to a creature so inferior as I.' Again, the implied author has trapped the reader. It isn't open to us to disbelieve utterly, only to express a qualified scepticism at travellers' tendencies to exaggerate. You are being created here as a reader who either believes entirely what Gulliver tells you, or has the impertinence to question him on matters of detail. That quiet little voice saying 'but I don't believe this at all' is all but silenced.

Read now chapter 11, returning to the questions posed at the beginning of the chapter, to wit (1) How do you view Gulliver's behaviour? and (2) What is the role of Pedro de Mendez?

DISCUSSION

(1) The ending might strike you as a quiet parody of the *Robinson Crusoe*-style ending for an imaginary voyage. Instead of the triumphant, uplifting flourish of a rescue, here we have Gulliver doing his best to avoid rescue, to the extent of running back into the jaws of danger. Ever since page 315, if not before, it has been apparent that Gulliver has been imitating the Houyhnhnms to an extent that the ordinary reader must find distasteful, even absurd. On page 325, he 'never presumed to speak, except in answer to a question, and then [he] did it with inward regret, because it was a loss of so much time for improving [himself]'. Can this degree of self-effacement be healthy? In literature narcissism (excessive self-love) has always been an unhealthy sign, but the kind of inverted narcissism that Gulliver manifests on page 327 seems even worse. It drives him to seek solitude, which was, to eighteenth-century writers, a very dangerous condition. One can dislike one's image, wish oneself more attractive and the like, without being in any kind of pathological state. To reject the evidence of one's essential humanity, however, to shun the society of one's own species, to imitate the manner of a horse, suggests a much more radical state of self-division. A standard television sit-com joke is to have a black person inveighing against immigrants. Gulliver's loathing of humans seems an even more comic version of that. How can he forget that he is one all the while? No reader can endorse Gulliver's treatment of his wife and family, or

his morbid disgust at propagation. I hesitate, however, to draw the conclusion that David Nokes does when he says that 'from now on we are in the mind of a madman. Gulliver's horror and detestation of the human body has finally led to a mental breakdown.'[16] This, again, is treating Gulliver as a novelistic character, with a convincing psychology, rather than as a satiric device designed to startle and vex the reader. (If Gulliver is a 'character', so must his wife and children be. Yet no-one thinks of them in this way. Rather, one thinks of them as introduced to intensify Gulliver's loathing of humanity to fever pitch, to the point where it is most vexing to the reader.) Gulliver has made the mistake that some readers also make. In a manner of speaking, he has misread the work in which he appears. He has regarded the Houyhnhnms as 'ideal' in the sense of being 'perfect or supremely excellent in kind' and 'answering to one's highest conception' (*OED* 2), rather than as 'ideal in the sense of existing as a rational archetype.' (*OED* 1). As a transcendent form of rationality, the Houyhnhnms have no connection with humans, other than to establish that humans do not correspond to this form. His trying to imitate them is perhaps ultimate evidence that Gulliver cannot think straight.

(2) On page 325, Gulliver provides one of his many catalogues of the evils of human society, which he is spared in Houyhnhnmland. Perhaps, though, the reader does not altogether endorse the point it makes. This catalogue, very much a cityscape, pulsates with energy. It gives a carnivalesque impression, in its randomness and lack of order. Gulliver's advent is clearly the only interesting thing that has happened to the Houyhnhnms in recent times, providing what is perhaps their first genuine debating point in Council. Readers may find themselves longing for just such animation as Gulliver's catalogue affirms. At all events, I cannot really endorse his verdict on humans, that they are 'Yahoos in shape and disposition, perhaps a little more civilized, and qualified with the gift of speech, but making no other use of Reason, than to improve and multiply those vices, whereof their brethren in this country had only the share that Nature allotted them' (p. 327). Yahoo Newton? Yahoo Handel? Surely not. And the introduction of Captain Pedro de Mendez as a character supports a much more sanguine view of human charity and kindness than Gulliver's cynical verdict would suggest. Mendez is not even an Englishman – he does not have even that advantage, or, presumably, the advantage of being a Protestant! Now, let's be quite clear about this. I am not saying that Mendez' existence proves that humans can act rationally. It does not. It does prove, to my satisfaction, that I should not endorse Gulliver's opinions or actions in Book 4, which is

to say, that I do not accept that humans are either Yahoos or Houyhnhnms.

SUMMARY

I intend to save discussion of chapter 12 for the last chapter, along with the book's introductory material (the 'Letter to Sympson' *et al.*). So I am in a position to summarize this chapter's findings now.

What I have just said may suggest that I take a 'soggy liberal' view of Book 4, to wit that I believe humans to be mid-way between Yahoos and Houyhnhnms, able to degenerate into brutes or, contrariwise, to aspire towards rationality, depending on how they regulate their behaviour. (We formulated this view, as proposition 1 above.) This is a very familiar Renaissance world-picture. It is also the view taken by some critics. Charles Peake, for instance, whose views on Gulliver as a 'character' I quoted with approbation in chapter 2: 'it does not follow that man is being identified as an irrational creature. Gulliver is as easily distinguished from Yahoo as from Houyhnhnm, and, in fact, is placed midway between them.'[17] But I don't think it is what one takes away from *Gulliver's Travels*. This is too static a view to take of a text which seems to me to be a dynamic work, a discontinuous, inconsistent aesthetic object that needs to be read detail by detail. Overall theories about its meaning — 'the Houyhnhnms represent . . .' or 'the Yahoos represent . . .' — tend to blind us to local complexity. So please bear that in mind when reading what follows. About the Yahoos, the discourse can make any one of three statements: man is a Yahoo, man is superior to the Yahoo, man is inferior to the Yahoo. All of these statements are in fact made, sometimes in very close proximity to one another. As far as the Houyhnhnms are concerned, I suppose I am closer to hard readers than to soft ones. Everything I know about Swift points to the conclusion that he did long for clarity and order, while recognizing that human emotions made it very difficult to achieve. I said of Lilliput that imagining this community offered Swift an opportunity to project clear-cut political division, where damaging intrigue and faction could be thrown into stark relief. In life, Swift devoted much energy to bridging the political divide between Harley and Bolingbroke, men who were supposed to be on the same side as Tories, but who opposed each other more effectively than they did the Whigs. One often senses Swift's bewilderment that strong personal antipathies could so muddy the waters of clear political action. For Swift, the Houyhnhnms are admirable — and this certainly shows a rigid, authoritarian side to his imagination.

Since biographical questions *have* been invoked here, it is appropriate to raise an issue that I have scarcely touched upon thus far. Some commentators on *Gulliver's Travels* have wished to say that as an Anglican clergyman, Swift could not possibly have intended the 'black' reading of the text to which I am inclined. His religious belief, so the argument would go, would have been incompatible with such deep pessimism about human rationality and the imperfections of human nature. Gauging the extent of Swift's scepticism is a task well beyond the limitations of this book and I can do little more here than record the conclusions that I have come to after many years of reading Swift. There is very little in *Gulliver's Travels* or anywhere else in Swift that reveals the nature of Swift's religious faith in its spiritual or sacramental dimension. As a churchman of the Church of Ireland, he was squeezed between Roman Catholics and Ulster presbyterians, a spokesman for a hard-pressed, seriously declining Establishment. As Louis Landa puts it, 'the story was always the same: too many Papists and too few Protestants; a scarcity of endowed vicarages; a great lack of churches, and of those in use many "far inferior to the Stables and Barns of our Gentry"; glebes and parsonages seldom to be found; non-residence, the rule rather than the exception'.[18] This miserable condition was one that Swift spent all his life combating, fiercely resisting any legislation that might worsen the temporal condition of the clergy. He could have gained little incentive for optimism here. Although he was a conscientious Dean of St Patrick's Cathedral in Dublin, and as a private individual extremely, if peculiarly, charitable, he did not perform the duties of a parish priest, and did not therefore require to spend time bolstering the faith of his ordinary parishioners, other than in his sermons. Those of Swift's sermons that have survived in print lead his recent biographer David Nokes to the conclusion that 'he found it impossible to believe he was actually required to love his neighbour'.[19] Certainly some strains of Christianity are compatible with pessimism. But there is some evidence to support the view that for Swift, the most that was possible was an outward practical conformity to the Anglican Church, which would conceal, or deflect attention from, real doubts about the fundamentals of faith.[20] There is a passage in *Gulliver's Travels* which I have always found chilling. In Brobdingnag, the King is amused by Gulliver's account of sectarianism in his own country:

> He laughed at my odd kind of arithmetic (as he was pleased to call it) in reckoning the numbers of our people by a computation drawn from the several sects among us in religion and politics. He said, he knew no reason, why those who entertain opinions prejudicial to the public should be obliged to change, or should not be obliged to conceal them. And as it was tryanny in any government to require the first, so it was

weakness not to enforce the second: for, a man may be allowed to keep poisons in his closet, but not to vend them about as cordials.

(p. 171)

In *Gulliver's Travels*, Swift was able to take some of his poisons out of the closet; but its harsh comedy ensured that he would never be accused of trying to sell them!

I have laid stress on reader-response theories of reading, because they foreground the kind of vigilant attention that is needed to recognize the traps Swift sets for us. However, I also think that the more we emphasize our own current responses to the text, the more we will tend towards 'soft' reading, while the more we emphasize authorial intentions, the more we will tend towards 'hard' reading. Those who think that the Houyhnhnms are ironized or otherwise undercut are trapped in the 'archive' (to use Foucault's term) of our own present-day response. But Swift does not make the mistake that Gulliver makes, of thinking them imitable. They are, when all is said and done, horses. Human emotional muddle and confusion such as Gulliver falls prey to is a source of regret to Swift, but it is inevitable.

In January 1728, Swift's lifelong friend (some say his wife), Esther Johnson, whom Swift called Stella, died. Swift was in England, soaking up the excitement caused by the publication of *Gulliver's Travels* in October 1726 while Stella's illness was worsening, and his letters witness his terror that he might have to return to Ireland and be present at her death. He even went the length of requesting that she be moved out of his Deanery, so that she should not breathe her last under his roof, or in front of his eyes. To many, this is a horrifying story of unnaturalness, or want of human sympathy. I don't think so. Readers of *Gulliver's Travels* will be familiar with the easy Houyhnhnm way of death (pp. 323–4), simply ceasing to be, in the Keatsian ideal. There are no emotional complications, no difficult and inadequate sermons about going to a better world, no rituals. This is what Swift seemed to long for, and what he knew was not possible. It was, I suspect, his certainty that he could not live up to this self-imposed ideal, his fear that his emotional nature would let him down, that led him to insist on Stella's removal from his vicinity. Saying farewell to her, he would have seemed like Gulliver taking leave of the Houyhnhnms.

5. The Satiric Frame

Please read now the last chapter of Book 4 and also the introductory
'Letter from Capt. Gulliver to his Cousin Sympson'. What functions
do they serve? Consider what bearing they have on the questions of
(1) Realism and (2) Colonialism. Look at the passage on pages
345–6 commencing 'My reconcilement to the Yahoo-kind' and
consider Gulliver's strictures on human pride.

DISCUSSION

I will start with the passage. Most commentators agree that, if there
is a connecting theme running through the entire work, it is that of
human pride. (Opinions vary on how far a consistent theme can be
said to impart 'unity' to the work.) Strategically close, then, to the
ending of the work, the reader is to be reminded of this predominant
concern: 'when I behold a lump of deformity and diseases both in
body and mind, smitten with *pride* . . .' Yet, as so often, the reader
does not get this message 'straight'. Gulliver has just given us a list
(yet another catalogue) of vices and follies 'which Nature has entitled
[us] to'. Obviously, however, this catalogue is not a catalogue of
'natural' follies, in any clear sense of the term. Most of them are
surely created by culture. Given that Gulliver is still stopping his nose
with rue, lavender and tobacco, that he insists on his wife keeping her
distance, that he spends much time looking in mirrors and that he
'pretend[s] to some superiority' over the rest of us (p. 342), he surely
cannot be free from the taint of pride that he identifies in others. This
unreliable narrator departs the work still fulminating in immodest
language about debased human nature, while his chapter professes
to assert the scrupulous accuracy and truth of his experiences.

On the subject of colonialism, most modern readers would wish
to applaud Gulliver to the echo. We have seen that throughout Book
4, questions are asked about how a mercantilist economics is complicated by the various colonial strategies designed to eliminate trading
competition by unfair means. Fuelling the anger on pages 342–4 is

Swift's direct experience of colonial exploitation in Ireland as well as his knowledge of scandalous chapters in history like the conquest of the Americas.

Yet in context, this question too is implicated in the larger question of realism. Why, if Gulliver was a discoverer of unknown lands overseas, did he not plant the British flag in them and claim them as dependencies, in the manner of the great Elizabethan explorers? This question is discussed as a potential challenge to the truth of the entire work. All the way through the work, Gulliver has anticipated scepticism and disbelief. In various ways, the discourse has tried to destroy the distinction between fiction and other forms of writing that can lay claim to factuality. Chiefly, the discourse has disguised itself as a travel book, a work that gives a non-fictional account of real events that actually occurred to a traveller still living. At various times, readers are invented by the discourse who might be inclined to challenge its veracity, though always within the limits of a frame supplied by the travel book itself. They are permitted to ask whether Gulliver might not be resorting to the kind of exaggeration habitual with travellers; but this, of course, strengthens rather than weakens its claim to be such a memoir. Three voyages end with the introduction of a figure – John Biddel, Wilcocks, de Mendez – who is constructed as being virtuous, and of good character, again designed to win the reader's confidence. 'Realism' is served by the difficulties Gulliver experiences in readjusting to home life. As we have seen, his disorientation is nowhere greater than in the fourth voyage, where it serves purposes beyond those of mere presentational realism. Figures are introduced, such as the map-maker Herman Moll, who really did live and whose actuality further complicates our sense of the fictional. In the final chapter, Gulliver asserts his willingness to have his work vetted by the Lord Chancellor and even takes a high moral tone over this, suggesting that it should become the condition for publication of all travel books. He cites a Latin tag, from Virgil's *Aeneid* 2.79–80, which when translated is seen to have a precise bearing on the fact/fiction dichotomy: 'nor, if cruel fortune has made Sinon miserable, shall she also make him false and deceitful'. In context, the Greek speaks the words to introduce an entirely false story. It is designed to persuade the Trojans to take the fatal wooden horse into their midst.

When we look beyond the strict confines of the narrative transaction itself, to the condition of publication of *Gulliver's Travels*, we find that this obscuring of the boundaries between fact and fiction continues. On 8 August 1726, the publisher Motte received from one Richard Sympson, supposed cousin to Lemuel Gulliver, a sample of his travel memoirs. Some little time later, the manuscript of the entire work was 'dropped at his house in the dark from a Hackney-coach'.[1] When it appeared, however, at the end of October, it was full of errors and heavily cut. Some non-authorial insertions were also made, much to Swift's fury. The 'Letter from Capt. Gulliver to his Cousin Sympson', one presumes, was written out of Swift's anger at seeing this cack-handed edition, though there is a theory that it was written for the later edition published by George Faulkner in 1735, where it first appeared. The letter goes well beyond expressing the author's disgust at this mangled text, however. Gulliver claims kinship with William Dampier, the universally known traveller, some of whose authenticity would therefore rub off onto him. Entirely disingenuously, the work claims to have no hidden allegorical significance and again proclaims its purpose of moral improvement. With comic-false-naiveté, Gulliver professes surprise that 'after above six months' warning', no moral reform has occurred. This allows him not only to complain at the various serials and keys that sprang up, but at the same time to remind the reader what a gigantic 'media event' the publication of the book was. From his position as grand old man, Gulliver is able to ride Swiftian hobby-horses, like the instability of language, its constant change and decay, while at the same time parrying criticism of his nautical accuracy. Even the secure 'facts' of the reading experience we have just undergone are sabotaged, as it is revealed that Brobdingnag is actually 'Brobdingrag'. This is oddly disturbing. Finally, rising up to his full moral height, Gulliver asserts that, elevated as he is by his contact with perfectly truthful beings, he is incapable of resorting to European deceit and evasion. As a way of complicating our sense of what is true and what is not, of what is fact and what is fiction, this is quite masterly.

Recent critical theory has stressed that there is no possibility of any direct literary reflection of 'life'. Grant Holly, in the course of a post-structuralist analysis of the work, calls attention to:

> its true beginnings which are false beginnings, its pseudonymous editors, publishers, friends of the author, its personae, its annotations, its systematic way ... of blurring the distinction between outside and inside, the world and the book, [which] attack[s] the illusions of the authoritative text, a signified which can escape the signifying process, and a commentary which is part of a different discourse from the work it comments on.[2]

What we call 'life' is itself made up of various kinds of representation, of a plurality of conflicting discourses. The distinction between fact and fiction is no simple business. In a recent stimulating book, Lennard J. Davis has argued that the novel was born out of a matrix in which 'news' – reportage of actual occurrences in the world

– was inseparable from fictional 'novels'. The discourses gradually separated as a result of certain ideological pressures which demanded a distinction between fact and fiction to be made.[3] Oddly, he does not discuss *Gulliver's Travels*, but it might be possible to see that Swift had powerful reasons for impeding this separation in the case of his own masterpiece. The book greatly complicates our easy apprehension of what is true and virtuous, while projecting an imaginary world in which truth and virtue would be instinctively available to all. This is its great – and truthful – achievement.

Appendix

Jonathan Swift (1667–1745): a 'Brief Life'

Swift was perhaps the most unlikely Irish patriot who ever lived. Irish born, living much of his life there, he was a disappointed man who spent much of his life regretting former glories. He was educated at the Kilkenny School and at Trinity College, Dublin, where he took an undistinguished B.A. in 1686. From 1689, he served as secretary to the illustrious former diplomat Sir William Temple on his estate at Moor Park, Surrey, where he conceived his early expectations of a prebend either in Canterbury or Westminster. In the event, after Ordination in 1694, he was presented to the ruined benefice of Kilroot in Co. Antrim in January 1695, which must have seemed an ironic mockery of his hopes. He returned to Temple's household until the latter's death in 1699, absorbing some of Temple's views of intellectual history and politics. In particular, he was influenced by Temple's opinions on the superiority of ancient to recent scholarship; and the intellectual in-fighting between the 'ancients' and the 'moderns' fuels his two major early satirical works published in 1704, *The Battel of the Books* and *A Tale of a Tub*. In Temple's household, he also met the most important woman in his life – some say his wife – Esther Johnson ('Stella'). For Stella he wrote his chronicle of the period 1710–14, when he could claim to have been at the centre of English political life, the *Journal to Stella*, as well as an accomplished series of birthday odes. Already, though, in 1696, he had 'proposed' to Jane Waring ('Varina'), albeit in terms so anaemic that she could not possibly accept! Later, in 1710, he began visiting Hester Vanhomrigh ('Vanessa') who remained devoted to Swift until her death in 1723; a death that the shock of his poem 'Cadenus and Vanessa', elegantly repudiating any suggestion that he was in love with her, is sometimes said to have caused.

When he became Vicar of Laracor and prebend of St Patrick's Cathedral, Dublin, in 1700, he would have been conscious that this was a gradual rise in rank, far from the meteoric progress he had expected. In the first decade of the eighteenth century, Swift was entrusted by the Irish Bishops with the mission of persuading the Whig government to relieve the Irish clergy of some burdensome taxes known as the First Fruits and Twentieth Parts. In this business, he received his earliest political education. The Whig hierarchy would not grant the favour unless they received support for their proposed abolition of the Test Act, the legislation of 1673 that debarred Nonconformists from holding state office. So in order to gain financial relief, Swift would have had to relinquish the only legislation that, in his view, protected the Established Church of Ireland from being swallowed up by 'Dissenters' and Catholics. When the Tories came into office in 1710, Swift was successful in gaining remission of First Fruits, thus embarking on his career as 'Hibernian Patriot'. Typically, his triumph became a disappointment when he failed to receive proper credit for it. Although Swift was intimate with all the eminent statesmen of the 1710–14 Tory ministry, he still missed the lucrative English patronage that, against the odds, he hoped for; and when he became Dean of St Patrick's in June 1713, his worldly race was run. Frustrated by the failure of his two friends Robert Harley, Earl of Oxford and Henry St John, Lord Bolingbroke to agree on anything and to build an effective Tory dynasty, Swift had to content himself with the self-importance of being a go-between. For that privilege, he had lost the friendship of Addison, Steele and other prominent Whigs. In the latter's *Tatler*, his poems acutely depicting London life, 'A Description of a City Shower' and 'A Description of the Morning' were published. Perhaps the most permanent legacy of that period was the influence on his later writing of the Scriblerus Club, a satirical society that Swift founded in company with Alexander Pope, John Gay, John Arbuthnot and Thomas Parnell. The targets identified by this association of wits, the projects they outlined and the techniques they devised were very influential, most obviously on Book 3 of *Gulliver's Travels*. On Queen Anne's death, and the fall of the Tories, Swift returned to Dublin, to what he considered exile. With the exception of two short trips to England in 1726 and 1727, when his political hopes were briefly renewed through his association with the Prince of Wales's Leicester House opposition to his father George I, and when he contributed to a burst of anti-Walpole satirical activity with the publication of *Gulliver's Travels* (October 1726), he remained in

Swift's Epitaph in St Patrick's Cathedral.

Ireland all his life. Despite the celebrity that *Gulliver's Travels* brought him, his English visits were not successful. The first visit was overshadowed by Stella's decline and death. Deafness, dizzy spells and Swift's anti-social temperament finally ruined the second trip, and he deeply offended Pope by fleeing his house in September 1727.

In his letters to English correspondents, Swift did not conceal his loathing of Ireland's parochialism and poverty. He wrote to Boling-broke that he feared dying in Dublin 'like a poisoned rat in a hole', and to Harley's son that he had been 'driven to this wretched Kingdom . . . by [his father's] want of power to keep me in what I ought to call my own Country; though I happened to be dropped here [in Ireland], and was a Year old before I left it, and to my Sorrow did not dye before I came back to it again'. Yet he was a fierce defender of the Irish people and inferior clergy, winning a deserved reputation as an Irish patriot in the 1720s that culminated in his gaining the freedom of the city of Dublin, and being deeply beloved by the Irish. His series of pamphlets known as the *Drapier's Letters* (1724) put paid to William Wood's hopes of making a fortune by compelling the Irish to accept huge mintings of debased copper coinage. Later, in 1729, Swift's frustration at centuries of colonial exploitation of the native Irish by English absentee landlords and conscience-free local gentry erupted in his most famous satire, *A Modest Proposal*.

To some readers, the scatological poems that Swift wrote in the 1730s, his intemperate satirical attacks on Irish politicians like 'Traulus' and 'The Legion Club', and his heavily ironic version of his own life given in 'Verses on the Death of Dr Swift' have seemed to be evidence of an incipient insanity that predated the Menière's syn-drome (an inner ear complaint) which tormented him in later life. Others have considered that his later works, the *Complete Collection of Polite and Ingenious Conversation* (1738) and *Directions to Servants*, are as trivial and disappointing as the later friendships with men like Thomas Sheridan and Patrick Delany, constrasting with the eminence of *Gulliver's Travels* and the august circle of Bolingbroke, Pope and Gay. I cannot endorse this verdict, either of his work or of the close friendships that enriched his parochial life. Samuel John-son's line in 'The Vanity of Human Wishes' – 'And Swift expires, a Driv'ler and a Show' – has perhaps been unduly influential as an epitaph on this great writer's career.

Throughout his literary career, Swift produced writing that does not comfortably accommodate the reader, offering the reader no secure position from which to respond to the text. He dismantles the ideological securities of his era, resisting attempts to impose the authority of unambiguous interpretations. Paradoxically, this uncertainty is produced by a prose style of metallic hardness and translucent clarity. Swift's texts, 'in constant retreat from their own certainties' (Ellen Pollak), gain from this a startling contemporaneity and modernism.

Notes

Chapter 1: A Voyage to Lilliput (pages 1–21)

1 In a recent book entitled *Factual Fictions* (Columbia U.P., 1983), Lennard Davis has argued that the novel developed from a 'matrix' in which factual news and novelistic fiction was scarcely distinguished. The critic C. J. Rawson, in *Gulliver and the Gentle Reader* (Routledge and Kegan Paul, 1973), has written well on the uncertainty of reader-response to Swift.

2 My account is based on the excellent discussion in Seymour Chatman, *Story and Discourse* (Cornell, 1978), pp. 126–34.

3 M. H. Abrams, *A Glossary of Literary Terms* (Holt, Rinehart, Winston, third edn, 1971), p. 4.

4 Arthur E. Case has gone furthest down the allegorical road in his *Four Essays on 'Gulliver's Travels'* (Princeton U.P., 1945) in which he argues, for instance, that Book 1 allegorizes the joint political fortunes of Oxford and Bolingbroke in the latter half of Queen Anne's reign.

5 W. A. Speck, *Stability and Strife* (Edward Arnold, 1977), pp. 222–3.

6 Henry St John, Lord Bolingbroke, *A Dissertation Upon Parties*, Letter XIX (1734).

7 See, for instance, J. A. Downie, 'Political Characterization in "Gulliver's Travels"', *Yearbook of English Studies* 7 (1977) and F. P. Lock, *The Politics of 'Gulliver's Travels'* (Oxford, Clarendon Press, 1980).

8 This argument is well made in Maureen Quilligan, *The Language of Allegory* (Cornell U.P., 1979).

9 Anyone who wishes to follow up this shift in 'discourse-formation' should read Michel Foucault, *The Order of Things* (1966, current English edition Tavistock Publications, 1985). This French historian's work is extremely influential on some strands of current literary criticism.

10 J. P. W. Rogers, 'Swift, Walpole and the Rope Dancers', *Papers in Language and Literature* 8 (1972).

11 William Dampier, *New Voyage Round the World* (1697), pp. 325–6.

12 J. C. Davis, *Utopia and the Ideal Society* (C.U.P., 1981), chapter 1.

13 Margaret Spufford, *Small Books and Pleasant Histories* (Georgia U.P., 1981), p. 34.

14 Frederick M. Keener, *The Chain of Becoming* (Columbia U.P., 1983), chapter 1.

15 See Louis Althusser, 'Ideology and Ideological State Apparatuses' in *Lenin and Philosophy* trans. Ben Brewster (London, New Left Books, 1971). I don't mean to imply that from his Marxist viewpoint, Althusser would endorse Swift's neo-classic account of 'corruption'. For him, the 'corruption' of which Swift speaks would be a corollary derivable from the same ideological formation.

Chapter 2: A Voyage to Brobdingnag (pages 22–46)

1 Shortly after the publication of *Gulliver's Travels*, Swift's friend John Gay's play *The Beggar's Opera* took the London stage by storm. Its songs and prominent images promoted an affably Hobbesian view of experience, concentrating on resemblances between seemingly civilized human behaviour and that of beasts. Swift himself used Hobbes's model in his poem *On Poetry: a Rapsody*, to provide a comic conceit for the way poets behave towards each other.

2 Aline Mackenzie Taylor, 'Sights and Monsters and Gulliver's *Voyage to Brobdingnag*', *Tulane Studies in English* 7 (1957).

3 J. Middleton Murry, in *Jonathan Swift: a Critical Biography* (New York, 1955) coined the phrase 'the excremental vision' for Swift's outlook in this respect. Norman O. Brown devotes a chapter to Freudian interpretations in *Life Against Death* (1959, rep. Sphere, 1968). And a recent biographer, David Nokes in his *Jonathan Swift, a Hypocrite Reversed* (O.U.P., 1985) finds 'ample evidence in both Swift's life and his works to accuse him of an anal fixation' (p. 372).

4 Carole Fabricant, *Swift's Landscape* (Johns Hopkins U.P., 1982).

5 For a fuller account of this mechanism, see Wayne C. Booth, *A Rhetoric of Irony* (U. Chicago Press, 1974).

6 See J. A. Downie, 'Political Characterization', cited above.

7 C. J. Rawson, in *Gulliver and the Gentle Reader*, cited above, has two exciting chapters on Swift's use of catalogues and lists. See chs. 4, 5.

8 Robert C. Elliott, *The Shape of Utopia* (U. Chicago Press, 1970), p. 55.

9 The passages are from Denis Donoghue, *Jonathan Swift: a Critical Introduction* (C.U.P., 1969), pp. 162–63; Charles Peake, 'The Coherence of 'Gulliver's Travels' in Claude Rawson ed. *Focus: Swift* (Sphere, 1971), p. 190; F. M. Keener, *The Chain of Becoming*, cited above, p. 89.

10 You can follow this up in W. B. Carnochan, *Confinement and Flight* (U. California Press, 1977).

11 Hopewell R. Selby, 'The Cell and the Garret' in Ronald C. Rosbottom ed. *Studies in Eighteenth-Century Culture* 6 (1977), pp. 140–1.

12 William King, *An Historical Account of the Heathen Gods and Heroes* (1711), p. 73.

Chapter 3: A Voyage to Laputa, Balnibarbi, Glubbdubdrib, Luggnagg and Japan (pages 47–76)

1 Ricardo Quintana, *The Mind and Art of Jonathan Swift* (1936, rep. Gloucester, Mass., 1965), pp. 315–16.

2   Quoted by Carole Fabricant, *Swift's Landscape*, cited above, p. 160.

3   If you want to find out more about seventeenth-century attempts to develop flight technology which may have some bearing on the Flying Island, consult Paul Korshin, 'The Intellectual Context of Swift's Flying Island', *Philological Quarterly* 50 (1971).

4   You can find out more about the Druids in *Encyclopaedia Britannica*, and in Stuart Piggott, *The Druids* (Thames and Hudson, 1983).

5   P. K. Elkin discusses this crucial critical debate in his *The Augustan Defence of Satire* (Oxford, Clarendon Press, 1973).

6   Di Marco Corolini, pseudonymous author of *A Key, being Observations and Explanatory Notes upon the Travels of Lemuel Gulliver* (1726) directs our attention towards this case.

7   The reader can find this reprinted in A. N. Jeffares ed. *Fair Liberty Was All His Cry: a Tercentenary Tribute to Jonathan Swift* (Macmillan, 1967).

8   Some have argued that the relationship between the Flying Island and the mainland in Book 3 allegorizes Swift's campaign, in 1724–5, to defeat the patent granted to William Wood to mint Irish copper coins. The interested reader can find accounts of this in vol. 3 of Irvin Ehrenpreis's authoritative biography *Swift, the Man, his Works and the Age* (Methuen, 1983) and might also want to read the pamphlets that Swift wrote which turned him into an Irish patriot-hero, *The Drapier's Letters*. I recommend the fourth of these entitled *A Letter to the Whole People of Ireland*. Is the Lindalino rebellion, chronicled on pp. 215–17 of the *Travels*, an extended reference to this issue? See also F. P. Lock, cited above, pp. 101–2.

9   The two cited passages are from Michael Hunter, *Science and Society in Restoration England* (C.U.P., 1981), pp. 17–18; and Joseph M. Levine, *Dr Woodward's Shield: History, Science and Satire in Augustan England* (U. California Press, 1977), p. 20.

10 See Jenny Mezciems, 'The Unity of Swift's "Voyage to Laputa"', *Modern Language Review* 72 (1977) for a sophisticated treatment of Bacon's influence on Swift.

11 To pursue the spider symbolism further, refer to Swift's early satirical work *The Battel of the Books*. An encounter between a spider and a bee dramatically symbolizes the quarrel between the Ancients and the Moderns, although with characteristically Swiftian ambiguity about who is in the right. On the ambiguity, see A. C. Elias, *Swift at Moor Park* (U. Pennsylvania Press, 1982).

12 'Hegemony' is a term used by the influential theorist Antonio Gramsci to mean not purely political rule but also domination of all forms of culture and of the dissemination of ideology – meanings and values expressive of class interest. Pat Rogers's article 'Gulliver and the Engineers' recently reprinted in his *Eighteenth-Century Encounters* (Harvester, 1985) should be consulted for the view that the world of 'projects' and 'projecting' depicted here is not exclusively that of the Royal Society, but is also the world of the newspaper columns and the patent office – an important supplement to Marjorie Nicolson.

13 A helpful book on the subject is Stephen K. Land, *The Philosophy of Language in Britain* (AMS Press, 1986).

14   Margaret Spufford, *Small Books and Pleasant Histories*, cited above, pp. 48–9.
15   I am indebted, for the information on the Atterbury Trials, to Edward Rosenheim Jr., 'Swift and the Atterbury Case' in Henry Knight Miller *et al.*, eds., *The Augustan Milieu* (Oxford, Clarendon Press, 1970).
16   Rosenheim, p. 193.
17   *The Works of Lucian*, trans. Thomas Brown (1711), 3.166–7.
18   Swift is quite close here to the philosophy of his contemporary Bernard Mandeville who, in the *Fable of the Bees* (1714, 1723), argued that commercial expansion depended on the indulgence of our appetites for luxury – 'private vice, public benefit'.
19   More information about Stowe can be found in Morris Brownell, *Alexander Pope and the Arts of Georgian England* (Oxford, Clarendon Press, 1978).
20   M. M. Kelsall, 'Iterum Houyhnhnm: Swift's Sextumvirate and the Horses', *Essays in Criticism* 19 (1969), 35–45.
21   William King, *Heathen Gods and Heroes*, cited above, pp. 6–7.
22   The interested reader might obtain the Penguin translation of Juvenal's tenth satire, or John Dryden's 1697 version, and compare the account given of old age with Swift's account of the ageing Struldbruggs.
23   This distinction was first made by the Russian Formalist theorists, where it appears as a distinction between *fabula/sjuzet*. It has gained wide acceptance. Gérard Genette, in his *Narrative Discourse* (current translation Blackwell, 1980), has developed the story: discourse relationship in sophisticated ways, some of which I make use of here.
24   Pierre Macherey, *A Theory of Literary Production* (1966, current translation Geoffrey Wall, Routledge and Kegan Paul, 1978).

Chapter 4: A Voyage to the Houyhnhnms (pages 76-104)

1   Frederik N. Smith, 'The Danger of Reading Swift: the Double Binds of *Gulliver's Travels*', *Studies in the Literary Imagination* 17 (1984), p. 35. F. R. Leavis's essay 'The Irony of Swift' (1934) is the landmark in this kind of criticism, and C. J. Rawson has been a leading exponent.
2   See, for instance, his *Is There a Text in this Class?* (Harvard U.P., 1980).
3   The sources of the passages cited are: (a) *The Correspondence of Jonathan Swift* ed. Harold Williams (Clarendon Press, 1963–65), 3.102–3; Kathleen Williams, *Jonathan Swift and the Age of Compromise* (U. Kansas Press, 1958), p. 198; Conrad Suits, 'The Role of the Horses in "A Voyage to the Houyhnhnms"', *University of Toronto Quarterly* 34 (1964/5), p. 128.
4   The terms 'hard' and 'soft' reading are coined by James Clifford in a very influential article, 'Gulliver's Fourth Voyage: "Hard" and "Soft" Schools of Interpretation', in Larry S. Champion ed. *Quick Springs of Sense* (Georgia U.P., 1974).
5   Frederic Jameson, in his *The Political Unconscious* (Cornell U.P., 1981), has brilliantly elaborated the idea that texts have a 'not-said', an 'unconscious', which the critic-analyst can bring to light, and which are

the results of certain kinds of repression of history. I am trying, perhaps ineptly, to make use of this idea here.

6   Michel Foucault, cited above, p. 131.

7   See Robert C. Gordon, 'Jonathan Swift and the Modern Art of War', *Bulletin of Research in the Humanities* (Summer, 1980).

8   An excellent introduction to the economic history of this period is provided in C. H. Wilson, *England's Apprenticeship, 1603–1763* (Longman, 1965). Specifically devoted to Swift's economics are Louis Landa, 'The Dismal Science in Houyhnhnmland', *Novel* 13 (1979); and Louis Landa, 'Swift's Economic Views and Mercantilism' in his *Essays in Eighteenth-Century English Literature* (Princeton U.P., 1980).

9   Swift was capable of producing more sophisticated accounts of what his friend Arbuthnot referred to as 'the art of political lying'. In *The Examiner* 14 (9 Nov. 1710), he says of the Duke of Wharton's political lies: 'he never yet considered whether any Proposition were True or False, but whether it were convenient for the present Minute or Company to affirm or deny it; so that if you think to refine upon him, by interpreting every Thing he says, as we do Dreams by the contrary, you are still to seek, and will find yourself equally deceived, whether you believe or no'.

10   Mercantilist providential philosophy is given poetic embodiment in Alexander Pope's poem *Windsor Forest*.

11   On Swift and Sparta, see Ian Higgins's excellent article 'Swift and Sparta: the Nostalgia of *Gulliver's Travels*', *Modern Language Review* 78.3 (1983).

12   The argument is made by J. C. Davis, *Utopia and the Ideal Society*, cited above.

13   This is the view taken by John Traugott in 'A Voyage to Nowhere with Thomas More and Jonathan Swift', *Sewanee Review* 69 (1961), p. 543.

14   For this extreme view, see Ann Cline Kelly, 'Swift's Explorations of Slavery in Houyhnhnmland and Ireland', *P.M.L.A.* 92 (1976); Donald T. Torchiana, 'Jonathan Swift, the Irish, and the Yahoos: the Case Reconsidered', *Philological Quarterly* 54 (1975).

15   Ralph W. Rader, 'Fact, Theory and Literary Explanation', *Critical Inquiry* 1 (1974).

16   David Nokes, *Jonathan Swift, a Hypocrite Reversed*, cited above, p. 326.

17   Charles Peake, cited above, p. 182.

18   Louis A. Landa, *Swift and the Church of Ireland* (Oxford, Clarendon Press, 1954, rev. 1965), p. 189.

19   David Nokes, *Jonathan Swift*, cited above, p. 277.

20   An interesting, if quirky, account of Swift's scepticism is to be found in Patrick Reilly, *Jonathan Swift: the Brave Desponder* (Manchester U.P., 1982), ch. 8.

Chapter 5: The Satiric Frame (pages 104–107)

1   Letter from Pope to Swift, 16 Nov. 1726.

2   Grant Holly, 'Travel and Translation: Textuality in *Gulliver's Travels'*
    Criticism* 21 (1979), p. 137.
3   Lennard J. Davis, *Factual Fictions: the Origins of the English Novel*,
    cited above.

Suggestions for Further Reading

Editions

All my references to *Gulliver's Travels* are to the Penguin edition, eds. Peter Dixon and John Chalker (rep. 1986). Several other editions are available, of which perhaps the best is that edited by Paul Turner (O.U.P., 1971).

    Other texts by Swift cited in my book are to be found most conveniently in the Oxford Authors *Jonathan Swift*, edited by Angus Ross and David Woolley (O.U.P., 1984), an excellently annotated compendium of Swift's writings. The standard edition of Swift's prose is Herbert Davis *et al.*, *The Prose Works of Jonathan Swift*, 14 vols (Blackwell, 1939–68). The best current edition of Swift's poetry is Pat Rogers ed. *Jonathan Swift: the Complete Poems* (Penguin, 1983).

Biography

In very recent years, three biographies of Swift have been published: the magisterial *Swift: the Man, his Works, and the Age*, 3 vols (Methuen, 1962–83) by Irvin Ehrenpreis; David Nokes's extremely readable if also intensely critical biography *Jonathan Swift, a Hypocrite Reversed* (O.U.P., 1985), available in paperback; and J. A. Downie's level-headed study of Swift's life in politics *Jonathan Swift: Political Writer* (Routledge and Kegan Paul, 1984). To my mind, Ehrenpreis's early book *The Personality of Jonathan Swift* (Harvard U.P., 1958) is not altogether superseded by the later biography.

Secondary Reading

Many suggestions for following up points made in the text are given in footnotes. They should be consulted for works of literary theory that have helped to shape my approach to questions of literary meaning, and for background studies of the period. Here I will confine my attention to books and articles on Swift. An annotated bibliography of recent Swift criticism is provided by Richard H. Rodino, *Swift Studies, 1965–1980: an Annotated Bibliography* (Garland, 1984).

Books

C. J. Rawson is perhaps the most sensitive recent critic on Swift, and his *Gulliver and the Gentle Reader* (Routledge, 1973) is indispensable. See also his 'The Character of Swift's Satire' in Rawson ed. *The Character of Swift's Satire: a Revised Focus* (Assoc. U.P., 1983), an altogether valuable collection. Anything Pat Rogers writes on the eighteenth century will be fascinating history, sociology or literary criticism and his recent *Eighteenth-Century Encounters* (Harvester, 1985) prints some of his essays on Swift. Other valuable collections of essays are: Frank Brady ed. *Twentieth Century Interpretations of Gulliver's Travels* (N.J., 1968); Norman Jeffares ed. *Fair Liberty Was All His Cry* (St. Martin's Press 1967); Clive T. Probyn ed. *The Art of Jonathan Swift* (Vision, 1978), from which I particularly recommend Angus Ross's piece on Swift as Hibernian patriot and David Woolley's remarkable study of Swift's own copy of *Gulliver's Travels*; Brian Vickers ed. *The World of Jonathan Swift* (Oxford, 1968). See especially Vickers's own piece comparing *Gulliver's Travels* to More's *Utopia*.

Other recent books on Swift include W. B. Carnochan, *Lemuel Gulliver's Mirror for Man* (U. California Press, 1968), one of the few book-length studies of *Gulliver's Travels*; Denis Donoghue, *Jonathan Swift: a Critical Introduction* (C.U.P., 1971), a powerful book; W. B. Ewald, Jr., *The Masks of Jonathan Swift* (Harvard U.P., 1954) is 'new criticism', well-deployed; Carole Fabricant, *Swift's Landscape* (Johns Hopkins U.P., 1982), a left-wing reading of his life and writing which is outstanding in the range of Swift's work covered; Ellen Pollak, *The Poetics of Sexual Myth* (U. Chicago Press, 1985), on Pope and Swift, certainly the best study of Swift and gender ever written; Herman J. Real and Heinz J. Vienken, *Jonathan Swift: "Gulliver's Travels"* (Munchen: Wilhelm Fink, 1984) for the reader who reads German, an excellent introduction with good annotated bibliography; Herman J. Real and Heinz J. Vienken eds. *Proceedings of the First Munster Symposium on Jonathan Swift* (Wilhelm Fink, 1985) is uneven, as conference papers are, but see Eric Rothstein's piece on the structure of *Gulliver's Travels*; Edward W. Rosenheim, Jr., *Swift and the Satirist's Art* (Chicago and London, 1963), which is useful in defining what the satirist thinks he is doing; Peter Steele, *Jonathan Swift: Preacher and Jester* (Oxford, Clarendon Press, 1978), a traditional approach, extremely well-written; Kathleen A. Swaim, *A Reading of 'Gulliver's Travels'* (Mouton, 1972) is very thorough and exhaustive; David Ward, *Jonathan Swift: an Introductory Essay* (Methuen, 1973) has a poor opinion of Book 3; Nigel Wood, *Swift* (1986), in the Harvester New Readings series at an affordable price; Everett Zimmerman, *Swift's Narrative Strategies* (Cornell U.P., 1983) for anyone who wants to follow up some of my points on narratology.

Articles

In addition to the articles mentioned in the footnotes, readers will find some value in the following. (Locating them is likely to require the resources of a good municipal or university library.)

Frank Brady, 'Vexations and Diversions: Three Problems in *Gulliver's Travels*', *Modern Philology* 75 (1978) is a witty setting-out of reading difficulties; Terry Castle, 'Why the Houyhnhnms Don't Write', *Essays in*

Literature 7 (1980) is very stimulating; R. S. Crane, 'The Houyhnhnms, the Yahoos and the History of Ideas' in J. A. Mazzeo ed. *Reason and the Imagination* (New York and London, 1962) has been more influential than any other single critical item on Swift; Margaret A. Doody, 'Insects, Vermin, and Horses: *Gulliver's Travels* and Virgil's *Georgics*' in Douglas Lane Patey and Timothy Keegan eds. *Augustan Studies: Essays in Honour of Irvin Ehrenpreis* (Assoc. U.P., 1985) is on a specific topic, but everything she writes is good; James E. Gill, 'Beast Over Man: Theriophilic Paradox in Gulliver's "Voyage to the Country of the Houyhnhnms"', *Studies in Philology* 67 (1970) covers a topic I have mentioned; Bertrand A. Goldgar, '*Gulliver's Travels* and the Opposition to Walpole' in Henry Knight Miller *et al.*, *The Augustan Milieu*, cited above. Useful for those interested in historical contextualization; A. C. Howell, '*Res et Verba*: Words and Things', *Journal of English Literary History* 13 (1946) treats this seminal topic in Book 3; Donald Keesey, 'The Distorted Image: Swift's Yahoos and the Critics', *Papers in English Language and Literature* 15 (1979) picks its way cautiously through the minefield of recent criticism; Ann Cline Kelly, 'After Eden: Gulliver's (Linguistic) Travels', *English Literary History* 45 (1978) is excellent on theories of language contemporary with Swift; John J. McManmon, 'The Problem of a Religious Interpretation of Gulliver's Fourth Voyage', *Journal of the History of Ideas* 27 (1966) is self-explanatory, and does a good job; Samuel H. Monk, 'The Pride of Lemuel Gulliver', *Sewanee Review* 63 (1955), a classic 'soft' reading; John F. Ross, 'The Final Comedy of Lemuel Gulliver' in *Studies in the Comic* (U. California Studies in English, 8 no. 2 [1941]) makes the important distinction between Swift and Gulliver; George Sherburn, 'Errors concerning the Houyhnhnms', *Modern Philology* 56 (1958) is influential on me as a 'hard' reader; W. E. Yeomans, 'The Houyhnhnms as Menippean Horse', *College English* 27 (1966) good on why we should not treat the text as a novel.

Index

This book is due for return on or before the last date shown below.